The Beautiful Roar

Forays into Amateur Choral Singing

The Beautiful Hour

The Beautiful Roar

Forays into Amateur Choral Singing

Keith Mitchell

AMHERST

ISBN 1 903637 26 0

Printed in Great Britain by
The Bath Press

First published in 2005 by

Amherst Publishing Limited
Longmore House, High Street, Otford, Sevenoaks, Kent TN14 5PQ

For Jared Armstrong

with gratitude for much patient
and time-consuming help.

Contents

The beautiful roar of the chorus under the dome.

W H Auden: *Spain*

Introduction

On 11th March 1998 *The Times* carried a report on a Mrs
Nadine Harrington who was asked by her 11-year-old
son's music teacher to take part in a choral concert at
Wells Cathedral. The teacher – at Millfield School in
Somerset – knew that Mrs Harrington was an amateur
choral singer; what he did not know was that she lived
at Alderwasley in Derbyshire, 189 miles away. But she
was not deterred. For several weeks she rose at 3.50 am
on Tuesdays and drove to the school, arriving at 8 am
for the weekly half-hour choir practice and leaving
immediately afterwards to get to work before lunch (as
well as being the mother of three, she is a director of the
family firm: Harrington Generators). "My husband
thinks I'm mad", Mrs Harrington said, "but it's worth
every mile, the distance and cost don't matter to me; it
is the achievement of singing at the cathedral. If any

opportunity comes along in life you have to grab it..."

Few of us are likely to copy so remarkable a display of enthusiasm and dedication by someone who is plainly a very remarkable person. Nevertheless, it probably represents a difference in degree but not in kind from that of most choral singers, who will turn out week after week, often on freezing or drenching winter evenings to tackle, say, the fearsome difficulties of the *Mass in B minor* (of which more is said later) or of getting one's tongue around the Hebrew text of Bernstein's *Chichester Psalms*. Why do they do it? Well, choral singing is uniquely satisfying, exhilarating, sometimes spiritually moving, always the most tremendous fun. Very few who have been involved are ever willing to give it up. At a very rough estimate, there are about a quarter-of-a-million amateur singers in more than 2,000 choral societies all over the United Kingdom; and in spite of gloomy predictions – often well founded – this amazingly strong tradition which has survived two world wars, the advent of television and other vicissitudes seems likely to keep going well into the 21st century.

As the sub-title suggests, what is offered here is essentially a collection of essays on various aspects of this luminous and valuable strand in the texture of

English musical life. There is an historical chapter, but the book is not primarily historical. Similarly, some remarks on choral technique are not meant to do duty for a proper manual of systematic instruction. I have in mind the kind of readers who like to reflect a little on what they are doing and perhaps to delve into it to satisfy curiosity.

The book is aimed primarily at members of medium or largish mixed choral societies which manage to get together an orchestra for a full-scale concert two or three times a year. Many will belong also to church choirs, 'single-sex' choirs and small, highly expert groups who sing mainly unaccompanied music; all of which are of course no less important, but they demand the kind of special treatment which is not attempted here.

1

Don't Shoot the Conductor
– with a note on singing

*Art begins with craft, and there is no art
until craft has been mastered.*

Anthony Burgess

Let it be said at once – and more than just said – let it be
proclaimed in the market squares and trumpeted from
the housetops, how much admiration, gratitude and
sympathy is due to choir directors who take on such
unpromising lumps of raw material as the average 'mixed
ability' choral society.

Take Miss White, who teaches violin at a fairly large
independent school. It has been 'one of those days'.
Arriving late (the car wouldn't start), she finds that the
key of the instrument cupboard is not in its usual place.
The head-teacher's secretary has a spare, but she is away

with 'flu, her deputy doesn't know where it is kept, and finding it takes about 20 minutes. During the lunch-break she learns that the PE teacher has in mind a Sports Day, the date of which clashes with a concert arranged many weeks ago in which her best pupils were to have displayed the results of a great deal of hard work and to which their parents had already been invited. Arriving home tired, dispirited and cross she then turns out, after a hasty supper, and drives several miles to a draughty church hall where she will rehearse, perhaps, a difficult piece of modern music which most of the choir have never sung before and on which very few of them have done enough homework. But they will expect of their conductor the most extraordinary skills and virtues: to be relaxed and humorous but not to waste time on too many jokes; to be occasionally stern but never ill-tempered or sarcastic; to grasp, on every page, in every bar, what the composer is aiming at and how and why the choir is falling short; to strive for perfection, but not to be depressed by the thought that it is unlikely to be achieved.

This last-mentioned ability: to strike a happy medium between perfectionism – which can be simply tiresome and destructive in an imperfect world – and an unacceptable lowering of standards, must be one of the trickiest things. How strict should voice-tests be? A line must be drawn somewhere, but who can say exactly where? 'Mixed ability', in this context, means very mixed indeed. Music and mathematics have often been linked in various ways but one link, or similarity, not sufficiently recognised and taken on board, even by educationists, is the enormously long scale of natural aptitude which applies in both subjects and which does not seem to be matched in any other. Children (or adults) can be a bit better or a bit worse than average in, say, history or geography; but there is no real comparison here with maths, where the range stretches from the hardly numerate who have difficulty in totting up a restaurant bill, let alone managing a 17½% VAT calculation, and extends upwards to the top end: the youngsters one reads about who take A-level maths at primary-school age, do brilliantly, and go on to degree courses at the age of about 14.

Similarly, in choral singing, take the difference between two singers whom we will call Mrs Black and Mr Green. Mrs Black, an alto, is not only a pillar of the Barchester Choral Society, she also sings in the kind of highbrow small group who can sight-read Byrd's 'Though Amaryllis dance in green' or Walton's 'Drop,

drop, slow tears' and sing them perfectly second or third time round. Mr Green has a fine tenor voice and plenty of enthusiasm, but when it comes to reading music, well, he can just scrape through a not-too-strict voice test but he is terribly unsure and lacking in confidence. 'Placing' the tenor note in an opening chord, for example, or managing any unusual interval is usually beyond him.

Between the two comes a pretty large mass of singers who know what they ought to do but have difficulty in doing it; whose sight-reading is mediocre and – a depressing experience – seems to get no better, or only very slightly better, with practice; who have to work out, or remind themselves of, the sort of thing the Mrs Blacks seem to take in their stride: "Oh golly, we're in F minor with a flattened D, so that D to G interval in the third bar is a tritone, not a perfect 4th..."

This 'mixed ability' aspect also means that even for a writer qualified to do so – which I am not – there is an inescapable difficulty in doling out advice and instruction on how to sing. What level of competence is the reader to be supposed to possess? However, a few rapid observations may be worth making, along the lines that the best sermons are usually those which remind us of uncomfortable truths we already know and which may indeed be fairly obvious. The uncomfortable truth about choral singing can be put in 12 very simple words: there is no substitute for knowing the notes and watching the conductor. Phrasing, intonation, breathing, expression etc. are of course essential: they make the difference between performing a work as opposed to simply getting through it; but they are secondary in the sense of being dependent upon this first indispensable rule.

It is important, too, to be able to *count* (which depends on watching the conductor, which depends on knowing the notes...). It would be interesting to take a statistical sample of amateur choral singers to find out what percentage of them do actually count the beats between their entries as opposed to relying on the other parts to come in at the right time. (It is worth noting here that church choir members who are used to singing Renaissance polyphony – Palestrina, Byrd etc. – are at a great advantage. In that kind of music, which usually consists of a whole series of overlapping and often syncopated entries, the notes are easy enough but the *time* can be very difficult; and so counting the beats can hardly be dispensed with.)

Returning now to choir conductors who – it has already been made plain – are a race apart, a superior breed, the salt of the earth. Most of them, too, are humble people; which is why I feel able to offer, with immeasurable diffidence, just one reflection: not on technique or musicianship – which would be ridiculous – but on something as experienced and noted over about 50 years from the second row of the second tenors; and again in the category of a truth which is obvious but too easily forgotten. This is: the importance of not biting off more than can be properly chewed.

It is a depressing fact, that when dismal failures or even dreadful disasters occur, as they do from time to time with even the best choirs, it is nearly always because this commonsensical rule has been ignored. Bach's *Mass in B minor* seems to be particularly at risk, for reasons which are, or ought to be, clear enough. It is a sublime masterpiece, immensely satisfying and exciting to perform; and all self-respecting choirs feel bound to attempt it sooner or later. The fact remains that it contains 15 choruses which take up no less than 140 pages out of the 200 in the Novello score. Seven of them are in five parts, with divided sopranos; one in six parts (*Sanctus*) and one in eight – for two four-part choirs (*Hosanna*). Most of them are difficult and some are very difficult indeed.

In March 1892, under the doleful heading 'The Bach Choir's worst effort', George Bernard Shaw let loose one of his most withering blasts of scorn and vituperation in a report on what must indeed have been a dreadful performance of this work. He speaks of "The buzzing and wheezing and puffing and all sorts of uncouth sounds which ladies and gentlemen unknowingly bring forth in the agonies of holding on to a difficult part in a Bach chorus". He goes on to say:

> An untrained singer can no more sing Bach's florid choral parts than an untrained draughtsman can copy a drawing by Albrecht Durer. The attempts of ordinary amateurs to make their way through a Bach chorus are no more to be taken as Bach's music than a child's attempt to copy one of Durer's plumed helmets is to be taken as a reproduction of the original.*

The last thing these remarks are intended to do is to discourage any choir from singing this great music; and it should be said at once that Shaw overstates the case (as he was rather apt to do). The B minor Mass *can* be sung by 'ordinary amateurs'; but it needs more than the

---

Music in London 1890-94: Constable & Co. Ltd.

usual nine or ten rehearsals. Shaw was almost certainly not exaggerating when he wrote, in the report quoted above, "The work only received about one third of the necessary rehearsal". Even if about half the choir have sung the work before and know the music pretty well, what about the other half? Can they be trusted not to turn the 'Cum sancto spiritu' fugue or the eight-part 'Hosanna in excelsis' into a blurry haze or a suety mush?

Handel is also at risk from the fixed idea: his music is easy and does not need much rehearsal. This is a half-truth. Apart from the fact that any music whatsoever is difficult to sing really well, nearly every Handel work includes at least one or two not-at-all-easy choruses. Examples are the eight-part 'He led them through the deep' in *Israel in Egypt* and at least three of the 20 choruses in *Messiah* – about which more is said in the chapter on Handel.

To give just one more example: Mozart also is usually not very difficult, but let any choir beware of taking on the great *Mass in C minor* – in the version as completed by Alois Schmitt – without adequate rehearsal (as I have known to happen on one disastrous occasion). Choral writing predominates in this work; and it is in a high degree difficult and demanding.

-0-0-0-

When the great Italian tenor Enrico Caruso was asked what were his favourite operas he replied "They are all hard work". This is the attitude – perhaps the only possible attitude – of the true professional. Amateurs are not quite in the same position: they sing mainly for their own enjoyment. Nevertheless, it is not uncommon for those who have sung in German choirs to admit that they welcome the greater seriousness and dedication usually found in Germany – so long as this is not carried to the extreme of grim earnestness; and that they find the attitude and atmosphere of English choirs tend to be just a little too relaxed and jokey.

Probably the truth of the matter is summed up by Anthony Burgess in his remark about the relationship between art and craft used as the epigraph to this chapter; and by W B Yeats:

It's certain there is no fine thing

Since Adam's fall but needs much labouring.

2

The Early Days

*Amusements which wean the people from
vicious indulgences are in themselves a
great advantage: they contribute indirectly
to the increase of domestic comfort, and
promote the contentment of the artizan.*

John Hullah

To say that English amateur choral singing as we know
it began in 1841 may sound like a highly suspect
simplification. As Conor Cruise O'Brien has so rightly
said, "Confusion is the condition in which history exists,
as distinct from the way in which we try to tidy it up afterwards." But it so happens that that year was marked by
key events in the lives of three remarkable characters who
pioneered the 'movement' – as it can certainly be called.

The most spectacular of the three – though not perhaps

the most important in the long run – was a German called Joseph Mainzer, who arrived in England in June 1841, aged 40. After false starts as a mining engineer, a Catholic priest and an opera composer he had achieved startling success in what was obviously his true vocation: that of teacher of singing to 'the masses'. In fact his classes in Germany and France in the 1830s attracted such huge numbers that the authorities became suspicious: any sizeable gathering of mainly working-class people was seen in those days as a potential revolutionary mob. The English authorities seem to have been just a touch more liberal, or at least less frightened. Furthermore, popular choral singing was favourably regarded by the Victorian upper crust as contributing to the moral and religious betterment of the working classes, as well as keeping them happy. It is amusing to compare the Anglo-Saxon pragmatism of the quotation which heads this chapter (from a minute to the Privy Council's Committee on Education) with the lofty idealism of Mainzer: "Man is a being endowed with a triple nature, physical, moral, and intellectual, and cannot, therefore, derive any true and enduring enjoyment from productions merely material".

At any rate, Mainzer established himself in England

with astonishing rapidity. Within only one year he had launched a fortnightly journal, *Mainzer's Musical Times and Singing Circular* (later taken over by Alfred Novello as the *Musical Times*); had published a book, *Singing for the Million*, which went to 18 editions in about four months; and had 20,000 pupils being taught by himself and his assistants in various schools and institutes in London. All this was achieved by a man who knew hardly a word of English and at a time when about a third of the male and half of the female population were illiterate.

In 1843 Mainzer was more or less head-hunted by the good burghers of Edinburgh and moved his operations to that city, where he stayed until 1849. A second move then took him to Manchester. Both these cities witnessed the same spectacular success. After being in Manchester for only six months, for example, Mainzer conducted a choir of 2,000 singers drawn from his own classes. He died two years later at the age of 50, presumably worn out by overwork.

What was Mainzer's secret? How did this German émigré inspire, in such a short time, what Dr Percy Scholes calls "an extraordinary wave of enthusiasm for choral sight-singing which, for a time, carried away the populace almost as did some of the dancing manias or religious manias of the Middle Ages"?* There seems to be no obvious answer. The best-selling *Music for the Million* does not, according to Dr Scholes, convey the impression of a well organised and effective book; and the mild sensitive bespectacled face caught in a surviving portrait does not appear to be that of a commanding personality, though one can perhaps sense 'hidden fires'.

In contrast to this, the pictures of John Pyke Hullah and John Curwen display the confident near-smile of the firm mouth and steady eyes, and the abundant hair curling back from a lofty forehead, which are characteristics of so many Eminent Victorians. These two great musical educators deserve more than the brief

*From *The Mirror of Music: 1844-1944* by Percy A Scholes (Vol.1) (Novello & Co. Ltd and Oxford University Press. 1947.) The present writer is much indebted to this book, which is recommended to any reader who wishes to explore the historical background in greater detail. It covers not only choral singing but all aspects of musical life in Britain, as reflected in the pages of *The Musical Times*. (There is even a chapter on 'The Art and Practice of Whistling'; and a photograph of Ebenezer Prout.)

mention which is all that will be attempted here. They were both 'in business' at the same time as Mainzer – Hullah was, in fact, an admirer of Mainzer's work – though both outlived him by about three decades. What might be called the 'key year' of 1841 saw the start of Hullah's own classes in London, and before the end of the next year the number of his pupils was estimated at around 50,000. In 1844 he was appointed Professor of Vocal Music at King's College in the Strand; and later on, after the 1870 Education Act, he became the first Inspector of Music in schools.

It was in 1841 too that John Curwen, a Congregational minister, attended a Sunday school conference in Hull where music for the young was discussed, and he was commissioned to explore the educational possibilities. This he did with remarkable thoroughness. In particular, although he did not invent it, he pioneered and championed the 'Tonic Sol-Fa' system of sight-singing and notation, which eventually triumphed over all other methods and endures to this day. (One of the methods it triumphed over was that of Hullah, with whom there was a certain amount of not very friendly rivalry. Hullah used a Continental system rather similar to Mainzer's.) Curwen also founded the educational music publishing firm of John Curwen & Sons (originally sub-titled 'Tonic Sol-Fa Agency'), the success of which was consolidated in 1885, when the Education Department made a grant for sight-singing in schools.

Curwen's success was not without its shadier side. It owed a great deal to the work of yet another pioneer, this time a woman: Sarah Jane Glover, who taught in a school at Norwich, where her father was a clergyman. Using an expanded and adapted version of the Tonic Sol-Fa system she effectively trained the children to sing in her father's church choir; and in 1835 she published her *Scheme to Render Psalmody Congregational*. Curwen pirated this book and published his own version of what was essentially Miss Glover's system, without her approval, in 1841. (It would have been different, one suspects, had her book been published under a masculine pseudonym such as – to quote a couple of famous examples – Currer Bell or George Eliot.) However, in later life Curwen repented of this male chauvinist piggery and made a long overdue acknowledgment.

Choral singing did of course exist in England before the appearance of these great pioneers. Hullah's minute to the Privy council – quoted at the start of this chapter – was written in 1839; and only two or three years later he could write, in a different context, that "In the northern counties of England choral singing has long formed the chief rational amusement of the manufacturing population" and goes on to say that "the weavers of Lancashire and Yorkshire have been famed for their acquaintance with the great works of Handel and Haydn." Halifax Choral Society – the oldest still in existence – was founded in 1817; the famous Huddersfield one followed in 1836. Nor was such activity confined to the industrial north of England. Elegant Brighton's Sacred Harmonic Society, for example, was founded in 1827; the London-based Society of the same name followed in 1832 and boasted 700 members by the middle of the century; and, going back to 1810, a choral society which called itself, rather quaintly, The Sons of Handel, started up in Dublin. A look at choral singing in general as apart from amateur societies will of course take us back still further: examples are the Three Choirs Festival, which dates from the early 18th century, the Madrigal Society and the numerous Catch and Glee clubs, which follow only a few decades later.

It seems to be true, however, that what Dr Scholes calls the "extraordinary wave of enthusiasm" dates from the 1840 decade. It is also beyond doubt that its impressive roll and rise were greatly helped – perhaps even depended upon – cheap paper and much more efficient methods of printing, both of which became available at about that time and which were brilliantly exploited by Alfred Novello, of the famous music publishing firm founded by his father, Vincent Novello, in 1811. The effect of Novello's enterprise is well summed up by the writer of an article in the *Musical Times* in 1865, who pointed out that the firm's cheap series of oratorios not only supplied the lively demand "but actually created a public of its own, by circulating, at the price of a commonplace ballad, the entire Oratorio amongst the audience."

How on earth did they find either the time or the energy for choral singing, for learning and performing great music by Handel and Haydn, those many thousands of men and women who earned a precarious livelihood by toiling for dreadfully long hours at repetitive work in dark satanic mills? Is it merely wishful thinking to see this as yet another striking instance of the triumph of the human spirit over conditions which, it might be assumed, would stifle it utterly? No, surely not. But it is also true that in the 1830s and 40s things were beginning to get just a bit better. Chinks began to appear in the hitherto solid dogmatic structures of *laissez faire* and the iron laws of supply and demand, unquestioning belief in which was so characteristic a feature of the Victorian age. This was the period of the Factory Acts, in particular the Ten Hours Bill of 1847. Although aimed at woman and young people in textile factories, its effect was to stop all work after ten hours, as the men were not able to carry on without them; and similar measures were gradually extended to other industries.

By the 1850s and 60s the combined effects of trade unionism, more humane legislation and the increasing prosperity of the country as a whole, which to some extent 'filtered down', the lot of the wage earner began to show a little improvement. Of course by modern standards conditions were still pretty grim for many – particularly for unskilled workers. But the worst days were over.

Certainly there was a continual, and astonishing, rise in the popularity of choral singing all through the second half of the century. By the time the great old queen died in 1901 there were, according to one estimate, close on 5,000 choral societies in existence. A salient feature of this period was the emergence of the great industrial cities as musical centres, often under the leadership of remarkable and highly gifted individuals; also, associated with this, the establishment of music festivals held at regular intervals – usually of two or three years – which were seen as a mark of the city's dignity and prestige. These were not confined to the very largest cities, or to the north of England: there were festivals, for example, at Bristol, York, Norwich and Chester.

To do full justice to all this very widespread musical activity would entail excessive length; it would also be extremely difficult to separate the choral element from the orchestral, which began to assume an equal importance. To take Manchester for example, its Vocal Society's interesting repertoire is mentioned later in this chapter, and the city could also boast Sir Charles Hallé's Cecilia Society; but its name became associated, as it has been ever since, with the famous orchestra founded by Sir Charles in the 1850s.

At the grave risk of invidiousness, a few landmarks can however be picked out. Birmingham's choral tradition can reasonably claim a special eminence. Its Festival Choral Society was founded in 1811 (the festival itself dates back to the 18th century). It commissioned, and first performed, two works which have lasted to this day as highly regarded items in the choral repertoire:

Mendelssohn's *Elijah* (1846) and Elgar's *Dream of Gerontius* (1900).

From 1849 to 1882 the choir and orchestra were directed by Sir Michael Costa, a versatile musician of Italian birth noted for his masterly handling of large choral and orchestral forces: the Birmingham choir numbered 300 and its orchestra 130. He also composed. Two oratorios written for Birmingham – *Eli* and *Naaman* – were once widely performed, but are now forgotten.

Probably it was the first-mentioned of these about which Rossini wrote to a friend in 1856: "Good old Costa has sent me an oratorio and a Stilton cheese; the cheese was very fine..."

Also demanding mention is Sir Henry Coward, who in the later part of the century founded the Sheffield Musical Union: a choral society with singers drawn mainly from Sheffield and Leeds. Sir Henry insisted on a high degree of dedication, discipline and hard work; and this certainly paid off. His choir achieved new standards, gained a wide reputation, and undertook foreign tours to countries as far afield as Canada, Australia and South Africa.

-0-0-0-

What did they sing, this great country-wide multitude of choral enthusiasts? Mainly, it seems, oratorios. The immense – indeed amazing – popularity of this type of composition was another salient feature of the Victorian scene. In the earlier days *Messiah*, *The Creation* and (after 1846) *Elijah* were the Big Three which formed the staple diet, at least as far as longer works were concerned. It is significant that during the period of the Great Exhibition: May to September 1851, the Sacred Harmonic Society gave alternate performances, totalling 31 in all, of these three works alone. Not that Mendelssohn's popularity depended only on *Elijah*. *St Paul* and the *Hymn of Praise* were performed nearly as often as that great old war-horse. Mendelssohn's place as second only to Handel in public favour seems in fact to have lasted out the century. It is not until the 1920s that we find him dropped down to fourth place (on the basis of numbers of performances of his works): overtaken by Bach and – interestingly – Elgar.

As for Handel, a rather similar pattern is discernible. Although *Messiah*'s pride of place remained unchallenged, a good number of the other oratorios were given frequent airings: notably *Samson*, *Judas Maccabaeus*, *Israel in Egypt*, *Joshua* (now virtually unknown) and, among other kinds of choral settings, *Acis and Galatea*, *Alexander's Feast* and the *Dettinqen Te Deum*. It was not until the 20th century that Handel enthusiasts began to complain bitterly of their neglect.

Exceptions to the general pattern are always interesting, and the fairly startling one provided by the Manchester Vocal Society surely deserves a brief tribute. This choir, founded in 1866, specialised in unaccompanied singing and did not shrink, apparently, even from the very formidable difficulties of 'Bach's six great Motets, Byrd's Mass in D minor' and 'Tallis's Song in forty parts.' The last-named is, of course, the great Latin motet *Spem in alium* for eight five-part choirs; but we can only guess at 'Byrd's Mass in D minor'. Probably it was the one in five parts. The reference to Bach is the first that has appeared in this chapter; but few readers, I would guess, will need to be told that in his own lifetime Bach was renowned as a virtuoso organist, but hardly known as a composer; that it was not until 1830 and 1845 that full editions of, respectively, the *St Matthew Passion* and the *Mass in B Minor* were published (in Germany); and that in spite of the efforts of Samuel Wesley, Mendelssohn and a few other enthusiasts to stimulate interest, his music remained, at least in England, largely unknown and unperformed until the last two decades of the 19th century.

Returning to mainstream popularity, the names of Spohr* and Gounod can hardly avoid mention: "The two great masters of odorous devotion", as Percy Young calls them, who "flooded the world with piety and lachrymosity". The numerous oratorios of both composers were hugely popular but are now very rarely heard; in which respect they differ markedly from Stainer's *Crucifixion*, which still crops up around Good Friday as it has been doing continuously ever since it first appeared in 1887. A comment of Samuel Johnson's on a minor but best-selling 18th-century poet can surely be applied, no less appropriately, to Sir John Stainer: "He pleases many, and he who pleases many must have some species of merit."

Nothing said above should be taken to imply that the choral repertoire of the time comprised *only* popular

---

*Readers may have noticed - and perhaps wondered at – the inclusion of Spohr's name among the seven other much more illustrious ones ranged around the front cover of the older Novello vocal scores. It later gave place to Purcell's (I am not sure exactly when).

classics by well known names. There was a strong demand for new music by contemporary composers. If this bald fact appears as startling – or even hardly credible – it is because we have all become habituated to equating the 'modern' with the recondite, the unattractive and the fiendishly difficult. We tend to forget that this has not always been the case and that the music-lover who really loves only music written by composers who have been dead for at least a hundred years is an exclusively modern development. (There is more on this in the chapter 'How it looks today'.)

Most choral singers possess old Novello vocal scores dating back to about the turn of the last century, handed down to them by grandfathers or great-aunts or picked up in second-hand bookshops; and a fascinating few minutes can be spent examining the list of works advertised in the back pages. I have one of these, carefully preserved: a grubby and scuffed but still impressive gilt-edged hard-covered *Elijah*. In approximate round figures, it lists works – mainly oratorios – by 150 composers of whom only about 30 could be described as at all well known: leaving 120 whose names are remembered, if at all, only by the compilers of musical encyclopedias. There are, of course, borderline cases. It is rumoured that Hamish MacCunn's *Lay of the Last Minstrel* is worth reviving. One has at least heard of Sir Frederick Gore Ouseley, and it is just possible that his *Martyrdom of St. Polycarp* would grip and entrance audiences at the Festival or Albert Hall. But who knows of Franz Wilhelm Abt or would care to guess what glories may await rediscovery in his *Fay's Frolic* or *Minster Bells*? Or what gem of purest ray serene may lie buried in the dark unfathomed caves of (at random) Alice Mary Smith's *Ode to the North-East Wind*, Thomas Anderton's *Wreck of the Hesperus* or Heinrich Hofmans's *Song of the Norns*? And might Sir Arthur Sullivan's *Ode for the Colonial and Indian Exhibition* turn out to be more than just a curiosity? (No, probably not; but his *Golden Legend* has some fine moments and is worth the revivals it occasionally gets.)

This does indeed appear as a dim and dismal period in British music. As far as one can judge from names alone, roughly half of the 150 composers listed were contemporary British – i.e. Victorians - and virtually all their work has disappeared without trace, excepting only the oratorios of Stainer and Sullivan mentioned above, to which should be added a handful of pieces by Stanford and Parry – a revival of interest in both of whom is a feature of the contemporary scene. (Parry's spacious setting of Milton's 'Blest Pair of Sirens' has always held its place as a favourite; but it is a short piece lasting only about 12 minutes.) At the turn of the century this darkness was, of course, chased away by the glorious blaze of the Elgarian dawn and, a little later, the lasting daylight of Holst, Vaughan Williams, Delius and many others.

Still just within the 19th century, any account of amateur choral singing would be incomplete without a mention of Samuel Coleridge-Taylor, whose *Hiawatha's Wedding Feast* (1898) brought him immediate and nationwide fame in his mid-twenties: an age at which Elgar was an obscure bandmaster at Worcester county asylum. The extraordinary popularity of this piece – it has been called "one of the most universally beloved works of modern English music" – lasted well into the 1930s; and it is still performed, though much less frequently. A brief tribute to Coleridge-Taylor as a man may not be out of place. The son of a Sierra Leone doctor, he suffered with patience the usual insults and rebuffs occasioned by his colour and, according to Grove's Dictionary, "saw it as his mission in life to help establish the dignity of the black man." He died in 1912 at the early age of 37.

It seems true on the whole that the golden age of English popular choral singing ended with the outbreak of the First World War; but some years before that the decline of the oratorio as an important musical art-form had begun to be apparent. It had been ailing, if not terminally ill, it could be said, ever since Bernard Shaw in 1888 described Parry's *Judith*, the big British musical event of that year, as "emasculated Handel and watered Mendelssohn"; or even earlier with the appearance in 1873 of Sullivan's *The Light of the World*: a work found by one critic to possess "hardly enough vitality even to be vulgar". It is probably significant that even the essentially conservative Elgar did not feel it worthwhile to tackle the third oratorio in the trilogy of which *The Apostles* (1903) and *The Kingdom* (1906) were to have formed the first two parts; nor did he wish his best known choral work, *The Dream of Gerontius*, to be described as an oratorio (though to what other category it can be assigned is not at all clear).

To sum up: it seems hardly possible to dissent from the view of most music historians that the predominance of the oratorio a century ago had a stifling effect on musical life and creativity; and that no tears need be shed over its virtual demise.

After the war had ended in 1918 there was, for the most obvious and most terrible of reasons, a severe shortage of male singers. Choral singing recovered before very long. But this takes us well into the 20th century – beyond the scope of the present chapter.

42

3

The Fall and Rise of G F Handel

*Handel blazed the trail for the whole of that
revival of mass singing which has played a
far greater part than anything else in our
musical history. Since his time mankind has
heard no music written for voices which can
even feebly rival his for grandeur of build
and tone, nobility and tenderness of melody,
scholastic skill and ingenuity and
inexhaustible variety of effect.*

Sir Thomas Beecham

Victorian religiosity squatted like a great toad on Handel's
music well into the second half of the twentieth century;
and although its clammy weight has at last been shifted,
the damage done to this composer's reputation lingers on
and will take another decade or so to repair. The process
of rehabilitation is, moreover, still being hampered by a

peculiarly English mixture of ignorance and snobbery which might be called the I-prefer-Bach syndrome.

To expand on this a little: there is a certain type of music lover – usually of the older generation – for whom the extolling of Bach at the expense of Handel is a mark of superior discrimination. "Handel? Ah, yes, but actually I prefer Bach..." This remark, or variations of it, uttered in a tone of maddening superiority, expresses an idea which seems to be deeply ingrained. It was either during or shortly after the Second World War that a music critic called Ralph Hill could tell the several million readers of the *Radio Times* that as a boy he was "taught to love Bach and despise Handel." Today, when the Handel renaissance or rediscovery is in full flood, when at least 60 versions of the oratorios and many of the operas are available on CD, it may be difficult to convince younger readers of the low ebb to which Handel's reputation had sunk, or the extent to which the bulk of his music was simply unknown: apart from *Messiah*, which has never wavered in popularity, most concert-goers were familiar with only the *Water Music* – six movements from it in a version for modern orchestra – perhaps a few other orchestral pieces, and a handful of songs from the operas and oratorios. As for choral societies, they occasionally tried out a Handel oratorio other than *Messiah*, but found usually that audiences were not attracted.

The first rift in this darkness was the appearance, in 1959, of a splendid book by the eminent Handel scholar Winton Dean: *Handel's Dramatic Oratorios and Masques** which made out a powerful and hardly refutable case that the Victorians' solemn, grandiose, reverential approach to Handel's music was based on a fundamental misunderstanding of his genius and bound to provoke the reaction which set in soon after the turn of the 19th century. "The composer was condemned for what his admirers had made of him, not for what he was." The immense popularity of *Messiah* combined with a total neglect of his immense operatic output, established the idea of Handel as a primarily religious composer of 'sacred oratorios', nearly all of which can be better described as Old Testament music dramas, the product of a cosmopolitan man of the theatre who had devoted 30 years of his life – that is, all of his youth and much of his middle age – mainly to writing Italian operas for the London stage. Winton Dean's impressive research tracked down nearly 600 oratorio performances during

---

*Oxford University Press.

the composer's lifetime, only one of which took place in a consecrated building (apart from charity performances given in the chapel of the Foundling Hospital).

Handel did of course write a certain amount of church music over the course of his long creative life: some interesting settings of Catholic liturgical texts during his visit to Italy as a young man; anthems for the Duke of Chandos's private chapel at Cannons, the Duke's vast mansion at Edgware; ceremonial pieces – of which the Coronation Anthems are the best known – for the births, marriages, coronations and funerals of the Hanoverian royals. While works such as these are hardly conducive to deeply-felt religious utterance, it is hardly true to suggest that Handel was incapable of any such thing. Some commentators are apt to talk too glibly about his "reflecting the humanistic spirit of the age", ignoring such things as the hushed awe-filled unaccompanied setting of the theologically central Pauline texts 'Since by man came death' and 'For as in Adam all die' in *Messiah*, or the tragic intensity of 'How dark, 0 Lord, are thy decrees': the great chorus which ends the second Act of *Jeptha*. It can be argued, too, that dramatic story-telling is a good way to do theology.

It remains true, however, that if we are thinking

primarily of religious music, Bach is a religious composer in a sense that Handel is not. Church music was his job, at least for the last 27 years of his life when he was employed as Kantor (music director) at the two main churches in Leipzig, where he was expected to provide cantatas for every Sunday and feast day – that is, a different one every week. He composed nearly 300, covering five years, of which 200 are extant; also the great Passion settings, the motets for double choir, and the B minor Mass (which is an exception in that Bach apparently wrote it to please himself: there is no record of any performance in his lifetime). Unlike Handel, who was self-employed and concerned to please a fickle public, Bach was writing for a captive audience. The Lutheran Sunday church service began at seven in the morning and went on for about four hours, including an hour-long sermon. The cantatas – most of which last between 20 and 30 minutes – must have been a welcome relief: even the arias where, as happens occasionally, Bach's inspiration dries up and one realises with a sinking heart that there is going to be a seemingly interminable middle section followed by an equally long *da capo* repeat of the opening...

Well, even great Homer sometimes nods. Thinking

of so many marvellous things in the cantatas: to take examples almost at random, the opening of No. 68 (*Also hat Gott die Welt geliebt*), or the aria 'Es ist vollbracht' in No.159 (*Sehet wir geh'n hinauf gen Jerusalem*); or the chorus 'Lie still, O sacred limbs' near the end of the St John Passion, it is apparent that this particular note is one which Handel rarely struck. But enough has been said to highlight what is surely a plain truth: that there is an enormous chalk-and-cheese difference between these two great Baroque masters, and that comparisons between them are largely ridiculous. They were, of course, both German, and they were born in the same year; but this has no real significance. Anthony Trollope and Emily Brontë were both English and were born within three years of each other. Yet nobody in his senses would make a critical comparison of two novels so unlike as *Barchester Towers* and *Wuthering Heights*.

It has already been stressed that invidious comparison with Bach was not the only reason why Handel's stock fell so low in the earlier and middle years of the 20th century: it was linked with a reaction against the Victorians' badly distorted approach to his music; to which reference has already been made. This was epitomized by the mammoth Handel Festivals held in the Crystal Palace on Sydenham Hill; mention of which is surely demanded in any account of the English choral tradition. They took place every three years (except during the 1914 war) for more than 60 years: from 1859 - the centenary of the composer's death – until 1923. The distinguishing note of the festivals was the hugeness of the forces employed, especially the choral forces: at least 2,000 singers. An often-quoted report on a sort of trial run of the festival held in 1857 records that the Hallelujah chorus, sung by that number of voices, could be distinctly heard from nearly half-a-mile away. It was "impressive beyond description" and, the writer piously adds, "sounded as if a nation were at prayer." As for the first full-scale festival in 1859, the *Illustrated London News* reported that a performance of *Israel in Egypt* attracted an audience of 26,826 people. They were probably better fed than were the ancient Israelites under the new king who arose over Egypt, as they consumed (the paper records) 19,200 sandwiches, 14,000 pies, 240 fore-quarters of lamb, 3,052 lobster salads, 600 lettuces, 40,000 penny buns, 25,000 tuppeny ones, 32,000 ices and 3,506 quarts of tea, coffee, chocolate.

Well, the Victorians had a lot of fun; and the great choruses for double choir in *Israel* must indeed have provided a unique kind of thrill, sung by two or three thousand voices under the enormous metal-girder and glass transepts of that amazing building (destroyed by fire in 1936). While nobody could want a return to that kind of Handel – as massive as the dinosaur and more obviously doomed to extinction – the pendulum has now swung too far in the other direction, with choirs of not more than about 20 singers producing what can best be described as an underwhelming effect. (More is said about this in the chapter 'Two Cheers for Authenticity'.)

But to return to our main theme: the rehabilitation of a composer described by the novelist Samuel Butler as "lofty, impassioned, tender, and full alike of fire and love of play".* To pick out just a few significant landmarks

---

*Butler, almost literally, worshipped Handel. He was an amateur composer as well as a novelist and wrote two imitation-Handel oratorios, one of which is based on a facetious libretto about two simple shepherds who have abandoned their flocks and fields and jeopardised their marital prospects by unwise speculation on the Stock Exchange. The work ends with a fugal chorus on the text:

> How blest the prudent man, the maiden pure,
> Whose income is both ample and secure;
> Arising from Consolidated Three
> Per cent Annuities paid quarterly.

in this process: Winton Dean's book has already been mentioned. It was certainly a landmark, but it is a very substantial and scholarly work appealing mainly, though not exclusively, to specialists and academics. As for actual performance of the music, one could mention the formation, in 1955, of the Handel Opera Society; and in 1963 the issue of a very successful LP recording of the four Coronation Anthems, with Sir David Willcocks conducting the choir of King's College, Cambridge. (*Zadok the Priest* was at that time the only one of the anthems at all well known.) Another example, to which a precise date can be assigned, was a fire-flashing performance of *Dixit Dominus* by Sir John Eliot Gardiner's Monteverdi Choir at a Promenade Concert on 1st August, 1974. Listening to the tumultuous applause by an audience which contained a high proportion of young people, one could feel that the Handelian New Dawn had indeed broken with a vengeance.

Worth mentioning too – jumping on two or three decades to the present day – is the ongoing enterprise of Messrs Novello, who are bringing out new editions of virtually all of Handel's choral works, including the shorter ones, an interesting example of which is *The Ways of Zion do Mourn*: a sombre and impressive funeral anthem written for Handel's friend and patron, Queen Caroline (This little-known piece lasts about 40 minutes and was originally intended to form the first part of *Israel in Egypt*.)

There is plenty of evidence, then, for a 'Handel renaissance'. But it is still possible to find, in any choral society, members of 20-or-more years standing who know *Messiah* and a few of the minor works but who have never sung, for example, the Nightingale Chorus and all the rest of the gorgeous stuff in *Solomon*, the Plague Choruses in *Israel in Egypt* or the intensely dramatic and tragic music in the last Act of *Saul*. It is surely not just a Handelian's special pleading to think this a sad deprivation and to make the point that if amateur choirs used to do too much Handel – which is probably true – his neglect in the earlier years of the 20th century was a dismal impoverishment of the musical scene.

It might also be called a disregard of our national heritage. While it is not exactly true to call Handel a British composer, he was a naturalized Englishman for the last 30 years of his life, and he lived and worked in this country without interruption from 1712 (when he was 27) until his death in 1759: a man by that time – as portrayed by Roubilliac's bust in Westminster Abbey – old, blind, fat and rather ugly; but a great prince of music.

-0-0-0-

Difficult though it is to say anything new about *Messiah*, some kind of 'special mention' does seem to be called for in view of the unique place this work has occupied in English choral singing for nearly two-and-a-half centuries. By now the point has been quite often made, but it still needs to be stressed, how untypical it is, how it differs from nearly all the other oratorios by being essentially reflective rather than dramatic. Moreover, among more than 20 other works presented by Handel 'in the manner of an oratorio' only one other, *Israel in Egypt*, has a Biblical text, and only *Theodora* a Christian theme.

Just one chorus seems inconsistent with the non-dramatic character of the work: 'He trusted in God' in Part II, where the choir does appear – as it often does in the Bach Passion settings – to be taking the part of the crowd; in this case of bystanders mocking the crucified Christ. Bernard Shaw waxed extremely sarcastic about the manner in which this is usually sung: not with savage shouts of derision but in a solemn reverential manner, at about half the proper speed, "as if a large body of the leading citizens, headed by the mayor, were presenting a surpassingly dull address to somebody." He is almost certainly right. But the 'one off' character of this chorus does present some difficulty.

As has been mentioned earlier, there are strong reasons for deploring the way over-performance of *Messiah* has led to the mistaken idea of Handel as primarily a composer of church music; but only snobbery pure and simple can lie behind any misgivings in regard to the popularity itself or any sneering references to a 'national institution'. The work is a sublime masterpiece, with inspiration throughout at an extraordinarily high level. There are moreover comparatively few numbers – three out of more than 50 – adapted from earlier works. There is, certainly, some faulty declaration, an egregious example of which is the wrong emphasis: "*For* unto us a child is born". Nevertheless, those who make much of Handel's occasionally inept setting of English words should be asked to try and think of 'I know that my Redeemer liveth' set to any *other* tune. Of the 13 arias, only the two almost invariably omitted: 'Thou art gone up on high' and 'If God be for us' can be called dull, or at least unmemorable. As for the 20 choruses, even those usually cut in Parts II and III are interesting and singable – perhaps not quite as striking or essential as the others, but it is a great pity never to include them.

Another unique though very different aspect of *Messiah* is the way it has been used for raising money, usually for charity. It seems that Handel himself was the first to exploit the work's popularity in this way. The music historian Charles Burney apparently inspected the records of the Foundling Hospital – the composer's favourite charity: he gives the exact figure of £6,935 as the sum raised by eleven performances at the hospital conducted by Handel in the later years of his life: equivalent, of course, to a much larger sum today.

The contemporary practice of 'scratch' performances – usually of *Messiah*, but often of other well known works – can hardly be welcomed without reservation. It can be argued that such performances do indeed provide substantial sums for good causes as well as harmless fun for those who take part; and that perfectionism can have an inhibiting effect. The opposite view is no less firmly based: that to perform great music without proper rehearsal is an insult to the composer and even to the art of music itself. It seems to boil down to the familiar question about ends justifying means.

With *Messiah* in particular, another objection can be raised against 'scratch' performances: they tend to promote the belief that the music is easy and that everybody knows it well. Neither of these assumptions is entirely true. The rapid choruses 'And He shall purify' and 'His yoke is easy' are *very difficult* to sing with clarity and precision: qualities which are not just desirable, they are absolutely essential if the music is not to fall dismally short of its proper effect. And in how many performances does the concluding 'Amen' chorus come as a feeble anti-climax instead of a triumphant finale? The singers are tired; and perhaps this great fugal chorus has been under-rehearsed due to failure to take on board that it is one of the most extended and difficult in any Handel work.

Finally, on a different tack and if a frankly personal hunch can be excused: the fugue in the Overture has always seemed to me particularly fine, with a well shaped and memorable subject satisfyingly worked out. How I would love to hear it played, not in the usual aggressive tum-TUM-titti-tum-tum sort of way, rather fast and with no dynamic shading, but sensitively, *allegro moderato* with the *moderato* stressed, and with each part phrasing away with its own tune. It might then actually sound like *music*... But it would, alas, be virtually impossible to do this with the severely limited orchestral rehearsal time usually allowed.

4

Two Cheers for Authenticity

*The past is a foreign country: they do things
differently there.*

L. P. Hartley: *The Go-between*

It happens so often, and so widely – in politics as well
as in music and the other arts, and even to some extent
in science and medicine: what at first appears as a striking
and valuable idea or discovery with revolutionary
implications gets taken up by the establishment and
becomes, within a few years, a stifling orthodoxy. A case
in point is the current obsession with authenticity in
musical performance. Although it focuses mainly on
orchestral instruments and on styles of orchestral playing,
choral music certainly comes within its orbit; and some
of the more extreme manifestations could be said, with
only slight exaggeration, to present a threat to the very

existence of amateur choirs. But there is more on this later. Let us first do justice to the positive side.

Nobody would wish to quarrel with the basic premiss: that the music of past ages can be compared to a great painting, the beauty of which has been spoilt by two-or-more centuries of dust, dirt and the injudicious application of varnish; all of which must be cleaned off so that the true colours can appear in their pristine splendour and with the effect intended by the artist. This idea has taken root to the extent that the changes it has produced are now largely taken for granted. It seems hardly credible, for example, that nobody knew what a counter-tenor sounded like before Alfred Deller appeared on the scene in the late 1940s. More recently than that, in the 1950s, Vaughan Williams was conducting performances of the *St Matthew Passion* using a piano, not a harpsichord, for the *continuo* part; and Thomas Beecham was re-orchestrating Handel in a manner reminiscent of Mantovani's Singing Strings. Later again, in the 1960s and 70s, one can recall performances of *Messiah* in which one, or perhaps two, of the four soloists would ornament final cadences, while the others would sing exactly what is printed in the Novello score. (This can still happen, though not very often. Ornamentation is always a tricky business,

Two Cheers for Authenticity

depending to some extent on individual taste and preference; and if overdone, or done badly, can be disastrous.
One can hardly blame some singers for funking it.)

Until quite recently, too, it was usual to have the
obbligato to the 'Benedictus' in the *B-minor Mass* played
on a violin rather than a flute; although the latter, as
Donald Tovey pointed out more than 50 years ago, was
probably what Bach intended. (He did not specify which
instrument was to be used, and the music lies within the
range of both.) Nevertheless, could not a decision on
this be left to individual preference? Nobody who has
heard Manoug Parikian's playing of this obbligato on
the older of Herbert Karajan's two recordings of the Mass
could possibly want that superb and uniquely Bachian
outline broken up by the flautist's pauses for breath.

A more solid and less disputable gain, now taken largely
for granted, is the practice of 'double dotting' adopted by
both players and singers in music of the baroque period:*

---

*Purists are apt to point out that 'baroque' is an architectural
term and that its application to music is, to say the least, questionable. Yes, but *convenience* cannot be entirely ignored. *How else*
is music written in the (exactly) 100 years between the birth of
Purcell and the death of Handel (1659 – 1759) to be briefly
described? (Applied to earlier – much earlier – composers such
as Monteverdi or Schutz the term can, certainly, be misleading.)

a dotted crotchet and quaver is almost invariably to be played as a double-dotted crotchet and semi-quaver. This does enhance so strikingly the vitality and interest of the music that one wonders how and why it took so long for the practice to become established. (Like anything else, it can be overdone. A case in point could be the overtures to Bach's orchestral suites; where, for a number of reasons, it seems doubtful whether a very pronounced double dotting either suits the character of the music or corresponds to what the composer had in mind.)

So far, so good. The trouble, the 'unacceptable face', the reason for withholding the third cheer, is that both performers and public tend to be too impressed, overawed, by scholars and musicologists; with the result that music of the baroque period and earlier is increasingly at the mercy of ideas which, to most music lovers, offer little beyond the interest of novelty and which provoke the question: can this *really* be what the composer intended?

An example of this tendency is the theory of the American conductor and musicologist Joshua Rifkin, that Bach's choral music should be performed with not more than one singer per part. Applied to some of the cantatas, the result can be more or less acceptable, even quite interesting; but when the two great settings of the Passion – St Matthew and St John – and the *B minor Mass* are treated in this way it is highly questionable. An authoritative, and more cautious, opinion on this is provided by Sir John Eliot Gardiner in the sleeve note to his fine recording of the *St Matthew Passion*. While he concedes, rather surprisingly, that Rifkin's one-performer-per-part theory is one that Bach "would surely not have considered improper, though far from ideal", he goes on:

> An opposite (and in my opinion more credible) view is held by the distinguished Bach scholar Hans-Joachim Schultze who concludes that "from the number and character of the original copies... the number of participants was no less than sixty" with the former students returning to "support this outstanding event".

The London Bach Choir is larger than what is indicated by Herr Schultze and probably larger than anything Bach envisaged; but it would be worse than ridiculous, it would be wretchedly ungrateful and mean-spirited, to dismiss or deride the performances of the *St Matthew Passion* given over a period of nearly 30 years by Dr Reginald Jacques when he was conductor of this choir. Hopelessly inauthentic they may have been by today's standards; but almost without exception, those who remember them, both singers and audience, bear witness to their deeply moving quality – one might call it a spiritual authenticity – which could not, surely, have differed in any important respect from what Bach intended.

Nor should we forget – but it seems in danger of being forgotten – that the kind of big choral sound produced by 200-or-more voices provides a thrilling experience not exactly matched by anything else. The same can be said of the effect of a choir of this size singing *softly:* the sound is unique and unforgettable. The neglect, the undervaluing, of this element of choral singing is one of the saddest and least defensible of the many sacrifices made on the altar of authenticity. (More is said about this later in the chapter.)

Even on the basic question of tempi we are too often brought up against what seems to be educated guesswork as opposed to certain knowledge. Does anybody *really know* what speed is implied by Handel's marking *Largo e staccato?* This is the tempo indicated for the chorus 'Surely He hath borne our griefs' in *Messiah.* I can think of at least one baroque music specialist who takes it at almost exactly twice the speed of Ebenezer Prout's metronome marking: quaver = 72 in the Novello edition. Yes, Prout is too ponderous; but surely this fine chorus should not be robbed of the weight and impressiveness which seem to be demanded both by the character of the music and by the theological centrality of the text: one of the great 'suffering servant' passages in Second Isaiah upon which much of Part II of the oratorio is based. It is worth noting, too, that the same *Largo e staccato* marking is used by Handel for the great double chorus 'The people shall hear' in *Israel in Egypt;* which nobody in his senses would attempt to conduct at a brisk trot.

The whole issue of tempo in older music is a vexed one; and it is true that the implications of, say, 'Andante' or 'Allegro' may have changed over the centuries. But would the basic meaning of 'Largo': slow, broad, have been largely ignored by Handel or by anybody else? It seems unlikely.

Where we do have some much more solid facts is on the question of early instruments and how they are to be played; facts derived from 18th-century textbooks widely accepted as authoritative: on keyboard-instrument playing by J S Bach's son Carl Philipp Emanuel; on violin technique by Leopold Mozart (his influential book appeared in 1956 – the year which saw the birth of his so-famous son Wolfgang Amadeus); and on the transverse flute by Johann-Joachim Quantz, who produced 300 concertos for this instrument in addition to his textbook (1752) on the method of playing it which went into several editions.

But the question still obtrudes: to what extent do early 18th-century instruments properly belong in the museum, and performances using them in the lecture room, rather than the concert hall? This point is made very strongly indeed by Roger Scruton in his fine and fascinating book *The Aesthetics of Music* (Clarendon Press, 1997). Professor Scruton's attitude to the whole authenticity movement is in fact marked by an uncompromising hostility. Its effect, he asserts, "has frequently been to cocoon the past in a wad of phoney scholarship, to elevate musicology over music, and to confine Bach and his contemporaries to an acoustic time-warp".

Discussion of instrumental music is of course tangential to the main concerns of this book, but perhaps we could pursue a little further just one particular example which illustrates very clearly the objections to an over-dogmatic approach to authenticity: Bach's keyboard music.

Nobody who has heard the recordings made half a

century ago by Edwin Fischer or more recently by Rosalyn Tureck, a fine and scholarly Bach player too little known outside America, could for a moment doubt the power and authority of their playing or feel that Bach's spirit and intentions were being in any serious way betrayed. And yet they both used modern pianofortes producing a sound which Bach certainly never heard and could probably not even have imagined (as did Glen Gould, another highly acclaimed Bach exponent – but too idiosyncratic to be cited as an example in this context). Let us by all means hear, and hear often, Bach's keyboard music played on authentic instruments. But to banish the piano altogether, as tended to be done in the 1980s and early 90s, is surely an illustration of what Roger Scruton, quoted above, means when he speaks of confining early music to "an acoustic time-warp". (More recently, it seems, sanity has returned to the recital platform and the dogmatic extremes are less often encountered.)

F R Leavis, the formidable Cambridge literary critic, used to tell students to "look at the words on the page"; as opposed, that is, to bringing to any work of literature a whole lot of extraneous preconceived ideas deriving from the author's life, cultural and historical background, reputation etc. So with music, surely, the important thing is, not exactly to "look at the notes in the score", but to get at the spirit of the music, at what the composer is trying to express rather than the exact means he might have used to express it. All of which could be seen as so obvious that apology is needed for stating it. And yet, looking at certain developments in the fairly recent past, it seems that nothing can be taken for granted.

The German musicologist and conductor Nikolaus Harnoncourt is widely and rightly respected as an interpreter of the music of the baroque period; and he has made a recording of the complete cycle of Bach's 200 surviving church cantatas. Nevertheless, when it comes to *Am abend desselbiqen Sabbats* (No. 42), may we not ask of Herr Harnoncourt: are you sure that the beautiful *sinfonia* which opens the cantata should be played in a jerky *staccato* manner with the phrases broken up into note-pairs? Would not a calm *legato*, be more appropriate to a piece which introduces a setting of the Gospel text for the First Sunday After Easter: a gathering, at evening, of the sad, bewildered disciples? "Then came Jesus and stood in the midst, and saith unto them, Peace be unto you." Surely Albert Schweitzer gets nearer to the heart of the music when he speaks of the "evening calm" which the composer is portraying. The point to be made here is that it is not only scholars, musicologists or professional music critics who are entitled to ask such questions. They can and should be asked by anybody who knows and loves the music of Bach and who recognises in it the expression of a deep religious faith.

How, then, and by whom, is it to be decided whether or not the experts are to be trusted? It is not being suggested that the findings of modern musical scholarship are to be simply ignored. The plea, again, is for commonsense – of the kind so well displayed in Professor Thurston Dart's remarks about the playing of ornaments in 18th-century music.

> Forty or fifty years ago no concert-performer bothered his head about them. Today some players still do not bother; others take some trouble to find out what they can about their correct performance; and a few fret and fidget unmercifully, losing their sense of proportion in a vain attempt to differentiate between the styles fashionable in Leipzig during January 1726 and those used in Dresden two months later. This is as absurd as fussing about how Latin was mispronounced by the choir at Cothën

when Bach was there, or trying to reproduce
Farinelli's vowel sounds.*

Where commonsense does certainly prevail and is
united with an almost unanimous desire to travel the
authentic road, is in a rejection of the heavy slow solemn
thick-porridge kind of singing into which nearly all
amateur choirs tend to lapse. Bernard Shaw called it
"the insufferable lumbering which is the curse of
English choral singing." He was thinking particularly
of Handel; and whatever has been said here about a too
rapid and lightweight treatment of one particular chorus
in *Messiah*, there is no doubt that Shaw was right to
deplore a 'lumbering' tempo in other parts of the work,
the effect of which is to make a brilliant chorus such as
'And He shall purify' "so dull that all the reputation of
Handel is needed to persuade Englishmen that they
ought to enjoy it, whilst Frenchmen go away from our
festivals confirmed in their scepticism as to our pet
musical classic."

It is not of course only in the music of Handel and of
the Baroque period that 'lumbering' is unacceptable. If
with the Romantic movement in general and the mid-

The Interpretation of Music, p.100 (Hutchinson)

19th century in particular a lightweight extrovert joyfulness is more rarely encountered than it is in Vivaldi, it is certainly not entirely absent. A particularly brilliant and memorable example is the 'Sanctus' in Verdi's *Requiem*: a fugue for double chorus in four-bar periods; but, as Donald Tovey points out, the effect is far from heavy or stiff, it is dance-like, and "the dance is that of the Sons of the Morning". An earth-bound lumbering simply will not do. Moving on to the 20th century (and at the risk of stating the obvious) the jazz-like syncopations in Constant Lambert's justly popular *Rio Grande* demand the kind of liveliness and precision far removed from the sort of thing Shaw was condemning.

To attempt a summing up: when they are based on half-truths, even very dubious generalisations can be difficult to refute. One such idea is that it is impossible for large choirs to achieve the kind of crispness and clarity which music of the baroque and classical periods demands. If this were true, or widely accepted as true, it would entail at worst a severe – and perhaps fatal – injury to the entire amateur choral tradition, and at best, a wretchedly inhibited approach to the tackling of such music by choirs of average or more than the average size: which is probably between about 80 and 120.

Difficult, sometimes very difficult, yes; impossible, no: this, obviously enough, is the vital distinction needed to sift out the truth from the half-truth. Its validity is attested by the fact that several of the best and most famous amateur choirs do in fact comprise a fairly large number of singers: around 150 is not unusual; and in none of them is the bad old tradition of Victorian stodginess encountered – even if they can sometimes be not quite unstodgy enough for some tastes. As for the dogmatic insistence that authentic performance is *ipso facto* precluded by choral forces of this size, it may be both instructive and interesting to take a look at what has been called "in some ways the most important single event in the history of English music during the 18th century": the Handel Commemoration held in Westminster Abbey and the Pantheon in 1784.*

---

*It was mistakenly supposed at that time that Handel was born in 1684; an error enshrined, as it were, in the inscription on the base of Roubillac's statue of the composer situated – rather high up – in the Poets' Corner in Westminster Abbey. The Pantheon was a large domed classical-styled building, with excellent accoustics, in Oxford Street. It was most unfortunately destroyed by fire and never rebuilt.

The music historian Charles Burney published a highly readable and entertaining account of what was an outstandingly successful event. He could never remember "so much curiosity excited, attention bestowed, or satisfaction glow in the countenances of those present, as on this occasion," and when for a moment or two he could tear his attention away from the music and the performers, he observed in the audience "nothing but tears of ecstacy *(sic)*, and looks of wonder and delight." The original plan was for three concerts: the first in the Abbey, comprising mainly excepts from the oratorios; the second, in the Pantheon, a selection of operatic arias and 'Grand Concertos' (from the Opus 6 set of 12); and the third back again in the Abbey for a performance of *Messiah*; but the two choral concerts were repeated by Royal Command.

Never before had so large a force of both singers and instrumentalists been got together: it is from this that the event derives its historical importance. Many of the performers, Burney tells us, "came unsolicited from the remotest parts of the kingdom, at their own expense." The choir comprised 59 sopranos (mostly boys), 48 altos (all men) and a startling number of tenors and basses: 83 and 84 respectively – a total of 274 singers. But it is the size of the orchestra which "makes one gasp and stretch one's eyes": a total of 250 players which included 157 strings and a massive woodwind section of 26 oboes and the same number of bassoons. Nor was the array of brass any less formidable: 12 trumpets, 12 horns and six trombones.

Whether we believe him or not, Burney is at pains to emphasise that the occasion was "no less remarkable for the multiplicity of voices and instruments employed than for accuracy and precision... When all the wheels of that huge machine, the Orchestra, were in motion, the effect resembled clockwork in everything but want of feeling and expression." He insists too that "Handel was always aspiring at numbers in his scores and in his Orchestra: and nothing can express his grand conceptions, but an omnipotent band. The generality of his productions in the hands of a few performers, is like the club of Alcides, or the bow of Ulysses, in the hands of a dwarf."

Would Handel have agreed? It is impossible to know, and futile to speculate. It may even be that the question did not greatly bother him. It *is* known that shortly before he died he conducted a performance of *Messiah* at the Foundling Hospital with a choir comprising 13 adult male singers and six boys (there were also six soloists, who may have joined in the choruses). But, with his essentially practical and pragmatic approach to music-making, would he not have used larger forces had they been available? And it does seem reasonable to suppose that Mozart must have had a fairly sizeable choir in mind when he said, of Handel, "He beats us all in *effect*, and when he so wills, he strikes like a thunderbolt."

What is certainly a fact, and perhaps a significant one, is that the 1784 commemoration took place only 25 years after the composer's death, and that many of the older members of the audience – including Burney, who was nearly 60 at the time – would have remembered perfectly well performances hardly more than a generation earlier conducted by Handel himself. Certainly the Victorians went ridiculously over the top a century later with their choirs of 3,000 at the Crystal Palace. But dogmatism, inflexibility, on the question of what forces are to be employed in the performance of baroque-period music does seem just a little unwise.

4

Gerontius and the Religious Paradox

In Peter Nichols' fascinating dark-grey comedy *Passion Play*, one of the main characters is firmly hooked on choral singing, and the desperate adulteries, recriminations and contretemps in which the play abounds are interspersed with startling fortissimo bursts of choral passages from the *St Matthew Passion*, *Messiah* and Verdi's *Requiem*; a telling device which is used to stress one of the issues raised more or less explicitly in the play: the prevalence of Christian art in a largely non-religious society. (The question whether, or in what sense, contemporary Britain can be described as a Christian country is relevant; but this is not the place to pursue it.)

It does seem a little odd, that so salient a feature of contemporary society should attract so little comment and appear indeed to be taken entirely for granted. Take the case of a tourist in almost any biggish European city. He may be an agnostic humanist or even a militant atheist; or he may, like so many others, have simply drifted away from religious belief. But he is a man of cultivated tastes, and feels nothing inconsistent about spending a day immersed in art of various kinds, of which the one common factor is an exclusively Christian inspiration. In the morning he inspects the cathedral and perhaps some other prominent church buildings. In the afternoon, at the art gallery, he experiences whatever emotions are appropriate when confronted with works so saturated with religious feeling as those of, say, Duccio, Fra Angelico or Piero della Francesca. And in the evening, at a concert at which Bach cantatas are performed, he is invited to meditate on texts expressing an intense Lutheran piety reinforced by the superb music to which they are set.

Leaving aside the question raised some years ago by Professor Edgar Wind, whether it is possible for anybody to respond adequately to such a rich and concentrated banquet of great art without suffering severe nervous exhaustion, what we seem to be faced with here is the widely accepted dogma of the irrelevance of subject matter. Yes, of course it is possible for non-Christians to enjoy Christian art. But can the subject matter be *so* unimportant? Does it make *no* difference? In relation to choral singing, let us remember that about four-fifths of the repertoire of the average choral society comprises works set to a Christian-religious text. Are we forced to the cynical conclusion that nobody pays any more attention to words and meanings than does – one suspects – the average hymn-singing congregation?

Even with devout Christians this same question – of words, subject matter – can arise, though on a slightly different tack; especially with the religious music of Haydn and Mozart. Some readers may, understandably, react with impatience or even hostility to any talk of problems and paradoxes in relation to this luminous and lovely music which has for nearly two centuries formed an indispensable part of the repertoire of every choral society in the land. But it does seem a little curious, the way a basic distinguishing fact seems to be entirely ignored: that with two notable exceptions: Haydn's *Creation* and *The Seasons*, we are dealing here with liturgical music: settings of the Eucharist or Mass, intended not for the concert hall but for actual use in church.* With music of this kind, the question does seem

---

*Bach's cantatas were also, of course, written for Lutheran church services; but they are not liturgical in quite the same sense.

to obtrude: were the Puritans *entirely* wrong to distrust the uneasy but inescapable alliance of art – particularly religious art – with pleasure? Not that the Puritans were alone in this. It has troubled all high-minded writers on aesthetics, on art and beauty, from Plato right up to the present day.

When Haydn was accused of making his church music too cheerful, that humble and deeply religious man replied: "When I think of God my heart leaps for joy." Yes, we can all respond to this; but there remains something 'not quite right' about setting the final prayer for peace, the *Dona nobis pacem*, to a jolly bouncing-along *allegro vivace*; as is done in what is probably his best known Mass, the 'Nelson' in D minor. This is, of course, only one example among many; it was the usual practice of both Haydn and Mozart, as if the appropriate fitting of music to the sense of the words was less important than sending the congregation home in a happy mood.

An important distinction must be drawn here between musical *language* and the musical *conventions* current at the time. That much of the church music of both Haydn and Mozart is composed in a language or style which could be roughly described as 'Viennese operatic' is not in itself a matter for regret. There is a clear and instructive parallel with Verdi, whose wonderful *Requiem* could certainly be called theatrical – too much so, the London critics felt when it was first produced in that city. But Verdi was simply using the musical language that came naturally to him; anything else would have been inconsistent with the depth and sincerity of his feelings. It is the *conventions* in place at the end of the 18th century – such as the 'happy ending' already mentioned – that provoke troublesome questions.

Another example of 'convention' rearing its unacceptable head is the dreadfully over-elaborate cadenza at the end of the 'Et incarnatus' in Mozart's great *C minor Mass* (K.427). The soprano soloist is given one of loveliest tunes Mozart ever wrote; but when at the end we come to the setting of 'et Homo factus est' – words expressing the most central and sacred mystery of the Christian faith – there is a cadenza lasting for 20 bars and accompanied by a concerto-like obbligato for two flutes. The distinguished critic and former editor of Grove's Musical Dictionary, Eric Blom, wrote that "it puts one in mind of the mad scene in Donizetti's *Lucia de Lammermoor.*" How can this be regarded as other than a blemish in a work to which the epithet 'great' is so justly applied? It is, furthermore, not at all consistent with the general tenor of the work, especially the choruses, which tend to be grandiose, austere and somewhat archaic in flavour.

It would of course be unfair and unreasonable to expect of these two great musicians, or indeed of anybody, that they should in all respects rise above, not be at all conditioned by, the cultural and social currents which were flowing so strongly at the time. Even if we cannot go all the way with Baron Friedrich von Hügel in his stern condemnation of "that atrocious thing, the 18th century – a purely *this*-worldly affair", it remains as true as such generalisations can ever be, that religion at that period of time was in a pretty bad way. If we think of how much splendid and entirely 'appropriate' music there is in the six great Masses composed by Haydn in the closing years of his life – they have quite recently come to be increasingly valued (and often sung) – and in Mozart's *Requiem* and the *C minor Mass* mentioned above, any reservations must be swallowed up in simple gratitude.

What, in any case, do we exactly mean by religious music? Can a clear line be drawn between the specifically religious on one hand, and the beautiful or 'numinous' on the other? The question is relevant and interesting enough to justify a brief digression, with examples illustrating the difficulty drawn from no further afield than the two famed masters of the late baroque period: Bach and Handel. The genuineness of Bach's Lutheran piety is not in question; and yet he could adapt, with very little change, odes written in praise of the Saxon Royal House for the 'Hosanna' in the *B minor Mass* and several movements in the *Christmas Oratorio.* And as for his great contemporary, generations of church organists have played a spacious tune known as 'Handel's Largo' under the impression that it is a religious piece instead of what it actually is: an aria from a near-comic Italian opera. For that, Handel can hardly be blamed. But the same composer's *Solomon*, although bearing the religious-sounding label 'oratorio', is in fact a gorgeous celebration of music, monarchy and sexual love in which the name of Jehovah just happens to crop up from time to time. One is almost ashamed to admit how hugely enjoyable it is to sing.

At the opposite extreme is Elgar's setting of Cardinal Newman's poem *The Dream of Gerontius:* a work which presents the 'religious paradox' in an acute and particularly interesting form. The work has been –

consistently for very nearly a century – one of the staple diet items of the amateur choral repertory, popular both with audiences and with singers; and this in spite of a text which deals not just in the basic Christian affirmations such as praise, penitence, thanksgiving, but which includes a number of distinctively Catholic doctrines: devotion to Mary, intercession of the saints, prayers and Masses for the dead, and the Nine Orders of Angels (though this is perhaps not distinctively Catholic – it comes in Milton). Purgatory, too, is included, and is indeed of some importance: it is where the soul of Gerontius finds itself in the closing pages of the work: a fact not taken on board by those – one quite often comes across them – who cannot understand why there is a quiet ending instead of a blaze of allelulias. No, heaven is promised, but not yet attained. "Swiftly shall pass thy night of trial here", the Angel sings, "And I will come and wake thee on the morrow."

On the work's first appearance the Irish Protestant composer and teacher, Charles Villiers Stanford, remarked that "it stank of incense"; and indeed, Christians of any denomination may react against the extremely wrought-up, intense and 'pious' atmosphere of *Gerontius*. All this tremendous holy fuss about one old man's death seems to contrast so strongly with Wilfred Owen's lament for that terrible slaughter of youth in the 1914-18 war:

>What passing bell for these who die as cattle?
>
>Only the monstrous anger of the guns...

There is nevertheless a solid theological underlay to what might be called the Catholic trappings; which most believers recognise and appreciate. Card-carrying agnostics or atheists, on the other hand, must find powerfully and explicitly Christian-religious works of this kind peculiarly exasperating; as must those who are able to take seriously Tillich's "source of ultimate concern" or Cupitt's "unifying symbol of the goals of our intellectual and moral life" (considered as definitions of God). As Miss Jean Brodie remarked about the Girl Guide movement: "For those who like that sort of thing, that is the sort of thing they like." They cannot like Newman's poem!

The circumstances surrounding the composition and first performance of *Gerontius* are of great interest, and a brief account is given here for the benefit of readers who may not be familiar with them. Newman's poem first appeared in the Jesuit magazine *The Month* in 1865 (a propitious year for imaginative literature: it saw the birth of Rudyard Kipling and W B Yeats as well as the publication of Lewis Carroll's *Alice in Wonderland*). The poem could well have been sub-titled 'A Vision of Death and Judgment', since this is what it is in fact about. It had haunted Elgar's imagination for many years; ever since he had been given a copy as a wedding present in 1889 by the parish priest of St George's, Worcester. At last, in 1900, the moment arrived and he produced his musical setting, after a summer of very hard work, in response to a commission from the Birmingham Festival.

Only about half of the poem was set. It does indeed suffer from the diffuseness which is the fault of so much 19th-century verse; and much of it lies dead on the page, as if quite literally waiting for the life-giving touch of Elgar's music. There are, for example, pages and pages of theological meditation by the Angel and by no less than five 'Choirs of Angelicals', who add a further *25* verses to the familiar six beginning "Praise to the Holiest in the height." With the help – perhaps the pretty considerable help – of his friend Fr Henry Bellasis of the Birmingham Oratory, Elgar did a masterly job of compression on all this, producing a much more compact narrative which retains the 'highlights' and gives scope for the variety of mood and expression which is so striking a feature of the music.

The first performance at Birmingham (on 3rd October 1900) was a disaster. Accounts vary as to exactly how much of a disaster, but it seems beyond doubt that an under-rehearsed choir and a stand-in conductor made a dismal hash of what appeared at the time to be difficult music in an unfamiliar idiom. The final rehearsal on the evening before the performance went on for six hours. It was attended by the composer himself, who lost his temper – a very bad mistake! – and it was a tired and dispirited body of singers who gathered for the Great Event the next day. One account of the performance records that at some points they went so flat that the orchestra played louder than they should have done in order to drown them out...

Almost crushed by disappointment and bitterness, Elgar wrote to a friend: "I always said God was against art... I have allowed my heart to open once – it is now shut against every religious feeling and every soft, gentle impulse *for ever.*" He could not, of course, have foreseen that Richter, the conductor at Birmingham, would take the work back to his native Germany and produce it with striking success during the following year, and that within a short time *Gerontius* would be acclaimed everywhere for what it is: a work of amazing power and originality, combining intensely personal utterance with absolute fidelity to the spirit of Newman's poem. Trouble over the text did, however, linger on for some years. In particular, the Chapters of Anglican cathedrals wanted to alter it to tone down the strong and distinctive Catholic flavour. But that was nearly a century ago. Nobody would now dare to alter a single word!

Without in any way detracting from Elgar's creative achievement, we could fittingly conclude by giving some credit where it is certainly due: to August Jaeger, Elgar's much loved and honoured friend immortalized, as 'Nimrod', by that most famous and most gorgeous of Elgarian tunes in the *Enigma Variations.* It is virtually certain that had it not been for Jaeger's skill and dedication as an overworked and (probably) underpaid editor at Novello's the manuscript score of *Gerontius* would not have been printed and ready in time for the Birmingham Festival.

Jaeger's contribution is well brought out in the fascinating collection of (Elgar's) *Letters to Nimrod,* edited by Prof. P M Young and published by Dennis Dobson in 1965. Apart from a great deal of humble but essential editorial donkey-work it seems that Jaeger was, in a sense, responsible for one of the most striking and memorable passages in the whole score: the orchestral build-up which precedes the moment when Gerontius is pierced by a brief glimpse of the Most Fair and utters his great and terrible cry: "Take me away..." Jaeger's own programme note describes it thus:

> The climax is prepared by the Judgment theme, given out, fully harmonised (and *what* harmonies!) at first over a pedal A, and rising by awe-inspiring steps, and, after a short pause, to one momentary *fffzp* on the chord of the thirteenth, which we must consider the composer's illustration of the Angel's promise: "Yes, for one moment thou shalt see thy Lord." At this point the composer's score contains the direction: "For *one moment* must every instrument exert its fullest force."

This, however, was not in the original manuscript score as Jaeger had received it. He writes to Elgar on June 15th (1900): "There is one page (159) I can make nothing of, i.e. nothing adequate to Newman's words or the situation, though I have played and sung it over and over again... Wagner would have made this the climax of expression in the work, especially in the orchestra... Heaven! What is your gorgeous orchestra for? And why should you be dull and sentimental at such a supremest *(sic)* moment?"

Elgar replied at first: "I *won't* alter p.159 & be darned to you"; but later he gives way: "I return the last proofs of the Thing: you are as usual, a brute to me. Will those bars do? You don't say. I can tell you one thing, old Mosshead: you might ask... or... or... to turn you out a few bars like that in vain! never mind. I'm glad I did it after all. I had in my original sketch marked it out so, but I thought it too much for the fat mind of the filistine *(sic)*. We shall see."

Well, yes, we *have* seen. We can also see, from the passage quoted above, that Elgar had no illusions about his own worth... But it is not difficult to forgive a little boastfulness in the composer of a work which, in the words of a priest at Newman's own Oratory at Birmingham, "grips its hearers wherever English is spoken and music loved, and to a faithless generation proclaims the reality of the invisible world."

6

Too Good to Miss:
Bach Cantatas Explored

One of the more extraordinary events of the year 2000 was Sir John Eliot Gardiner's 'Bach Cantata Pilgrimage' celebrating the 250th anniversary of the composer's death. Beginning on Christmas Day 1999 at the Herderkirche in Weimar, Sir John's Monteverdi Choir performed, over the whole year, all the near-200 extant church cantatas on the precise liturgical dates for which they were composed, in about 50 churches, abbeys, priories and cathedrals all over Europe. On the Continent, the choir's amazing tour began in Saxony, visiting the towns and churches where Bach worked, proceeding northwards towards Lubeck and the Baltic coast and eastwards through Denmark, Sweden, Finland, Estonia and Latvia, then west to Holland, France and Great Britain, where performances were given in such far-flung places of pilgrimage as St David's Cathedral in

Pembrokeshire, the abbey church of Iona in Scotland and St Magnus in Kirkwall, Orkney.

About half way through the tour, in August 2000, Sir John recorded: "One source of constant amazement during this tour is the sheer variety and beauty of the music: week after week Bach surprises us with one masterpiece after another"; and he goes on to praise what he calls the human qualities of Bach's compositions, his professional pride in his craftsmanship "tempered by his profound devotion and humility".

He does not exaggerate. The cantatas are full of the most gorgeous music; they comprise moreover by far the largest part of Bach's creative output, and not to know them is not really to know Bach. But it is also true that when it comes to performance of the cantatas by ordinary amateur choirs as opposed to top-ranking professional groups such as the Monteverdi, there are difficulties: real enough, but not insuperable.

The aim of this chapter is to touch on some of these, and in particular to recommend and briefly describe a selection of four cantatas which seem to me to be especially worth performing.

Here, I must admit, I am skating on fairly thin ice; and I proceed with much caution and diffidence, aware that many choir directors and choral society committees will know as much or more than I do about the cantatas and will have their own favourites. But then, who knows, or can be expected to know, *all* the extant cantatas? And I plead the further excuse, that although I am writing from a frankly personal angle – which I hope the reader will forgive - my selections are not purely arbitrary, based only on my happening to have known and loved the music for about 40 years.

On a more objective level, the works selected embody at least one feature which makes them especially suitable for performance: they give the choral singers plenty to do. While I cannot entirely go along with the late Sir Jack Westrup when he calls the solos and duets "the chief glory of the cantatas" it is true that a great many of them – about 100 in fact – begin with an extended opening chorus after which there is nothing else for the choir to sing except, at the end, a simple four-part setting of one verse of a chorale – in which the church congregation in Bach's time would be able to take part. I have avoided cantatas of that type.

Nor are my selections entirely unknown: at least one of them, No.21, used to be performed quite often. But this whole question of popularity is a tricky one. It is probable that the handful of cantatas which might be called popular appeal more to listeners, to buyers of compact discs, than to singers. An exception to this, certainly, is No.140: *Wachet auf, ruft uns die Stimme* which is possibly the best known and loved of all Bach's church cantatas, full of beautiful things in addition to the superb and unforgettable counter-melody to the chorale known as "Zion hears her watchmen's voices"; as satisfying to sing as it is to listen to. But No.147: *Herz und Mund und Tat und Leben* seems to me a different case. I suspect that its popularity derives almost entirely from another even more famous counter-melodied chorale: the one set to English verses by Robert Bridges beginning "Jesu, joy of man's desiring". The rest of the music does not seem to me to represent Bach at his most inspired.

Proceeding now to my recommendations without further preamble: all are for four-part choir; other details, namely, approximate duration, soloists and orchestration are given for each cantata. As for the music itself, there is some comment and description, but no detailed analysis.

BWV 63: CHRISTEN, ATZET DIESEN TAG
Duration: 30 minutes. Soloists: SATB
Orchestra: 3 oboes - 1 bassoon - 4 trumpets -
timpani - strings - continuo.

This is an example of what might be called the Festival
Cantatas: it was written for Christmas Day and was
performed in 1723 – the year in which Bach started his
job as Kantor in Leipzig, where he was responsible for
the music in the city's main churches and where he stayed
for the remaining 27 years of his life. From the point of
view of most non-professional choirs, the advantage of
this type of cantata is that the sizeable orchestra required
will not be submerged by a fairly large number of singers.
There may of course be difficulties with expense,
particularly where Bach asks for special instruments
which are used in perhaps only one movement in the
whole work. But surely, no orchestra of the Baroque
period can be called large when compared with what is
needed for many 19th-century works, let alone more
recent ones such as Schoenberg's *Gurrelieder* or
Walton's *Belshazzar's Feast.*

On a rather different tack: the opening words of
Cantata No.63 do certainly raise the question of whether

to sing in the original German rather than an English translation. *"Christen, ätzet diesen Tag in Metall und Marmorsteine!"* Englished freely to produce the same number of syllables comes out as "Christians, etch this blessed day in rich bronze and glowing marble!" Is this really singable? In general, some choir directors have strong opinions on this question, and one hesitates before taking a too decided or dogmatic stand on either side. Perhaps simple commonsense is the best guide. Brahms's *Ein deutsches Requiem*, for example, certainly goes better in the original German; but to learn and to sing this fairly long work in a foreign language does make heavy and time-consuming demands. (It is shaming to note that German choirs seem to take singing in English as a matter of course and to do so without apparent difficulty!)

The case is different, though, with Bach cantatas. Most of them are comparatively short and there is usually a certain amount of *da capo* repetition; in view of which it seems not unreasonable to ask singers to desert Shakespeare's language and learn just a little of Goethe's. For those who nevertheless demand a translation, the series of all the cantatas brought out by the German publishers Hanssler is strongly recommended:

everything is very clearly printed, with the English text in italics to avoid confusion with the German (which is in roman). Accompanists will be glad to note that the piano arrangements "have been adapted first and foremost with the player in mind" and that "chords which are impossible to play have been avoided"(!).

Focusing again on this particular cantata, No.63: the joyful opening chorus spreads itself over nearly 300 bars – taking into account the *da capo* repeat of the first 120 – in 3/8 time and in Bach's most fluent and singable contrapuntal style. After an alto recitative extolling the wonder of the Incarnation comes the first of the two duets (there are no solo arias – an unusual feature): for soprano and bass, on the theme of trust and gratitude. In spite of the attractive oboe obbligato this rather lengthy number seems to me to outstay its welcome. With the two voices so widely separated the higher one can sound cruelly exposed. (But this may well be simply a personal non-preference.)

In contrast, the second duet (alto and tenor) which follows after a recitative is entirely captivating, dancing along in 3/8 time. Schweitzer recommends perusal of this duet to "anyone who thinks that Bach cannot write in an agreeable popular style". After a fully accompanied and strikingly imaginative bass recitative we have the final chorus which exceeds even the opening one in sheer magnificence, not without subtle and interesting touches: five bars of unaccompanied choral writing at the start of the fugue which follows the grandiose opening; and a middle section unexpectedly interrupted by a brief *adagio* episode as the choir implores deliverance from Satan's threatening power.

It is worth putting on record that when the Monteverdi Choir performed the cantata at Southwark Cathedral in December 1998 Sir John Eliot Gardiner *encored* this chorus in response to enthusiastic and prolonged applause: certainly an unheard of thing in Bach's time, nor would it be acceptable today in the context of a church service. But in the public performance of a festive-type cantata it seems to me to get by.

BWV 68: ALSO HAT GOTT DIE WELT GELIEBT
(God so loved the world)
Duration: 20 minutes.   Soloists: SB
Orchestra: 2 oboes plus 1 oboe da caccia (or cor anglais) - 1 horn - 3 trombones - strings (including solo violoncello piccolo - see below) - continuo.

This is one of the cantatas Bach wrote for Whit Monday. With its smaller scale and its quiet, reflective mood it offers a very complete contrast to the exuberance of *Christen ätzet diesen Tag*, and is perhaps unsuitable for choirs of more than about 50 singers. The opening chorus is unusual: in 12/8 time throughout, with a gently swaying Siciliano rhythm and D minor tonality. The effect produced is one of combined gravity and beauty.

The soprano aria which immediately follows used to be one of Bach's best known and most often performed solo pieces: *"Mein glaubiges Herze"* – "My heart ever faithful"; but it is now rarely heard, such are the vagaries of musical taste and fashion. Startling, perhaps even shocking, to learn that the aria was adapted with not much alteration from a secular cantata written ten years earlier for a hunting festival held to celebrate the birthday of Duke Ernst Wilhelm of Weimar. Bach was unwilling to 'waste' the long - nearly 30 bars - of orchestral *ritornello* which ends the movement. A violoncello piccolo is specified, which may cause some difficulty; but there should be ways around this.

It is probably true that the appeal of this cantata derives from its first two numbers and that neither the second aria, for bass, nor the final chorus have quite the same appeal. As for the chorus, it is unlikely that any composer would be inspired by the negative tone of the text. But in common with nearly all of Bach's music, this austere fugal movement is both challenging and satisfying to sing.

BWV 11: LOBET GOTT IN SEINEN REICHEN
(Praise God in his kingdom) - Ascension Oratorio
Duration: 30 minutes. Soloists: SATB
Orchestra: 2 flutes - 2 oboes 1 bassoon (optional)
- 3 trumpets - timpani - strings - continuo.

'Ascension Oratorio' is Bach's own title, and something of a mystery, since three other cantatas celebrating this feast have come down to us. Perhaps it is because it contains several passages of recitative taken direct from the Gospel narrative and sung by an 'Evangelist'. Be that as it may, the title is an advantage, fixing in the memory both the work itself and the day in the Christian calendar for which it was written. The cantata is in two parts: the sermon would have come between them in the Lutheran church service.

A powerful and resplendent opening chorus is followed by a short tenor recitative: Jesus blesses his disciples "and is parted from them" (Luke 24:51). "Ah, Jesus, must you go so soon?" the bass soloist laments: a theme taken up by the alto in one of Bach's most moving arias. It is moreover one which everybody will recognise as an earlier version of the *Agnus Dei* in the B minor Mass where it appears with some modifications and in a different key.

After the Evangelist has recounted how a cloud obscured Jesus from sight, Part I ends with a simple chorale.

Part II opens with some short recitatives completing the Gospel narrative, after which the soprano soloist sings an aria of serene beauty to a text which speaks of refreshment of spirit and a foretaste of future glory. The aria is supported only by instruments in the higher range: flutes, oboes, violas and violins; and the whole movement seems to float in the air half-way to heaven.

Although the final movement is essentially a homophonic setting of a hymn-tune it is aptly described as a choral fantasia rather than simply a chorale, supported as it is by an elaborate and extended orchestral accompaniment. Here I must admit to a strong personal attachment: the trumpet tune which recurs throughout has always seemed to me one of the most splendid and exhilarating Bach ever wrote: Schweitzer describes it as "glowing with an ardent, mystic love". When will the day dawn, the hymn-writer asks, when we shall greet the Saviour? As if uncertain of the answer, the chorus part ends, as it were inconclusively, in the relative minor (strange that no commentator seems to have picked up so unusual a feature); but the effect is to make the orchestra's final return to D major all the more satisfying.

BWV 21: ICH HATTE VIEL BEKUMMERNIS IN
MEINEN HERZEN (My heart is sorely troubled)
Duration: 45 minutes. Soloists: STB
Orchestra: 1 oboe - 3 trumpets - 4 trombones
- timpani - strings - continuo

While this used to be one of the better-known cantatas,
I have the impression that in recent years it has fallen
into neglect; which is a pity, because choral writing
makes up a sizeable proportion of the three-quarters of
an hour of music, nearly all of which is at a high level of
inspiration and originality. There are in fact four choruses
(no chorales). One's feeling that there is 'something
special' about this work seems to have been shared by
Bach himself. The liturgical date is the Third Sunday
after Trinity – the Gospel reading is the parable of the
lost sheep in Luke XV – but the score is marked 'per
ogni Tempo' (for any season).

Like the Ascension Oratorio, the work is divided into
two parts. It opens with a Sinfonia in which the oboe,
joined by the first violin, weaves wandering arabesques
suggesting the lostness of the lost sheep: sad, but most
beautiful – it is sometimes played as a 'self-contained'
orchestral piece. The choir then enters with a fairly

sombre fugue, the mood of which changes to liveliness and joy as the troubled spirit is refreshed by the Lord (the text is based on the 19th verse of Psalm 94).

Grief and anguish return with a soprano aria and a tenor recitative, both of which are moving and expressive, as is the succeeding aria in which the tenor declares himself "cast adrift without a rudder, sail or anchor".

The chorus which ends Part I is in the form of a prelude and fugue; the prelude is full of striking and original touches; the fugue perhaps rather conventional and less interesting.

Sorrow and sighing are banished in Part II, which begins with a duet in the form of a dramatic – almost operatic – dialogue between the soul and its Comforter, sung respectively by the soprano and bass soloists. "Come, my Jesus, quicken and restore me". "Yes, I will come", the Saviour replies. The long chorus which follows is based on a verse from Psalm 116 which enjoins restfulness and contentment of soul. The slowly rising and descending scales of the main theme are interwoven with verses from a 17th-century hymn set in long notes and sung first by the tenors and then by the sopranos. The gradual unwinding of Bach's majestic counterpoint conveys the effect of a wonderfully sonorous 'build-up'.

A short and joyful tenor aria is followed by the final chorus based on the text from Revelations made familiar by its use in Handel's *Messiah:* "Worthy is the Lamb that was slain". A massive chordal prelude – it could in fact be described as Handelian in its breadth and harmonic simplicity – is followed by an exciting fugue, the full orchestral accompaniment to which includes fanfares played by the three trumpets.

In conclusion, it might be as well to come down from the lofty heights and take a brief look at the brass tacks or nitty-gritty of actual performance. The fact, or at least the strong possibility must be faced that except perhaps in large cities a programme consisting only of Bach cantatas would have too limited an appeal to be financially viable; and this is not suggested. The course often followed is surely the obvious and sensible one: to use a cantata to fill in, to make an evening's music, when the main item is one of the many in the standard repertoire that last for less or not much more than an hour. It could provide a memorable experience for both singers and audience.

7

How It Looks Today

The passions, whether violent or otherwise, must never be expressed to disgust – and music, even in the most terrific situations, must never give pain to the ear, but ever delight it and remain music.

Mozart, in a letter to his father (1781)

The idea that there is a kind of duty or moral obligation to try and 'appreciate' music, or art of any kind, which holds no appeal for us, which gives us no pleasure, is one of the more tedious and ridiculous heresies of our age; so too is its equally unacceptable corollary: the artist or creator regarded as absolute king of the castle, obliged to please nobody except himself and feeling able to adopt towards his audience or public an attitude of lofty indifference, or even of contempt. This monstrous tyranny seems, moreover, to be so widely accepted, regarded as a norm, as to be hardly ever challenged in any serious or effective way.

Acts of rebellion do, however, erupt from time to time. One of the first and most striking of these occurs in the introduction to *All What Jazz*, a collection of jazz record reviews, by Phillip Larkin, published in 1970.* This trenchant and brilliantly written piece bitterly attacks the way traditional jazz was taken over and ruined by the highbrows in the years following the war. At about that time, Larkin writes, books about jazz began to strike an "oddly familiar" note: "This *development, this progress*, this *new language* that was more *difficult*, more *complex*, that required you to *work hard at appreciating it*, that you *couldn't expect to understand first go*... Of course! This was the language of criticism of modern painting, modern poetry, modern music."

So much for the symptoms; but what about the diagnosis? At the risk of over-simplifying a complex question: perhaps the basic trouble is that the decay of religious belief has left a gap which the arts are supposed to fill. They are, as the American critic Lionel Trilling put it, "no longer required to please" but are "expected to

---

*Reissued in *Required Writing* - Faber & Faber, 1983

provide the spiritual substance of life". Our thinking is influenced, too, by the insidious logical fallacy of the 'undistributed middle'. It may be plain enough that not every animal is a cow simply on account of having four legs; but it seems to be widely assumed that because, for example, the French Impressionists' exhibitions originally attracted dislike and derision it follows that anybody who can run inked bicycle tyres over a large canvas and offer the result as art is to be taken seriously because he may be acclaimed as a genius by future generations. An exaggeration? Hardly, in view of some of the items currently on display at the Tate and other galleries.

Although this book is not simply about music as such, a chapter on the modern scene can hardly fail to take into account recent developments as they affect amateur choral singing. Music, too, of all the arts, provides the clearest example of the enormous and damaging gap which has opened up between what a very small minority of specialists 'appreciate' (and possibly even enjoy) and what most people want and expect art to provide. The worst period was probably the 1960s, 70s and 80s, when the atonal or serialist music of composers such as Boulez and Stockhausen was taken up by the establishment and became what one commentator has called "a prevailing orthodoxy which exerted a Stalinist grip" – especially on sources of public subsidy. Young composers needing a grant from the Arts Council or who hoped to get their music performed at the Proms or on Radio 3 were obliged to adhere strictly to the atonal line.

It was against this background that amateur choralism came to be regarded by the establishment as a hopelessly conservative influence; as if to perform music which gave pleasure to both the singers and their audience was something to be ashamed of.

It is important to bear in mind that it is not only the ignorant, the lazy and the Philistine who dislike and reject the rebarbative products of so many modern composers; nor is it true that such dislike arises simply from the novelty of the works or a failure to understand them. As a distinguished composer, Anthony Milner, has put it:

> With very few exceptions, the works produced
> by serial techniques continue to be disliked both
> by the vast majority of what are so often
> condescendingly (and contemptuously) called
> 'ordinary music lovers' and by the majority of
> professional musicians young and old, despite
> the fact that some of these works are now more
> than half a century old.

Dr Milner goes on: "I write 'disliked', not 'misunderstood', for it is perfectly possible to know this kind of music well and yet continue to detest it".

What is presented here is not an argument for the creation of pot-boilers or a suggestion that we should all rest happily in a secure and complacent middlebrow anti-modernism which never strays off the beaten track. Of course an avant-garde is needed; the trouble comes when it is advanced to so great a distance as to be virtually out of sight.

Luckily, however, not all recent music is in this category – taking 'recent' to mean roughly the last three-quarters of the 20th century there is plenty of choral music which although 'challenging' is still accessible, which "remains music". William Walton's *Belshazzar's Feast* which first appeared in the early 1930s (it was later revised) is a good example of the sort of thing I mean: a piece which broke new ground, which is both difficult and uncompromisingly 'modern': the old dears and the Chapter Canons in the cathedral cities were shocked and thought the work unsuitable for performance at the Three Choirs Festival. But here again there was never any question of its being recondite, inaccessible. This brilliant and powerful music was soon firmly established in the repertoire of every choral society.

Still focusing on British music in the earlier half of the 20th century, Ralph Vaughan Williams is surely a name to be remembered in the context of amateur choral music: throughout his long life he both conducted amateur choirs and wrote for them such splendid large-scale works as the *Sea Symphony, Five Tudor Portraits, Dona Nobis Pacem* and *Hodie* – which actually appeared shortly after the turn of the half century. Elgar's *The Apostles* and *The Kingdom* were both written by 1906 but they belong essentially to the 19th-century oratorio tradition. *Pace* Sir Adrian Boult, who ranked *The Kingdom* above *The Dream of Gerontius*, I would rather single out *The Music Makers* (1912), the last of Elgar's choral works (apart from a patriotic war piece: *The Spirit of England*) . This work has suffered from critical under-estimation on account of the extensive – and quite startling – use made by the composer of ideas from previous works: in particular the famous 'Nimrod' tune from the *Enigmas Variations*. When one considers how often self-borrowing occurs in the work of both the two great baroque masters, Bach and Handel, this hardly seems sufficient reason to denigrate, not perhaps a masterpiece, but a work offering 40 minutes of vintage Elgar.

There are of course a number of other substantial works of the pre-war period that have gained a more or less secure niche in the repertoire: among them, still with British composers, Holst's *Hymn of Jesus*, Dyson's *Canterbury Pilgrims*, Lambert's *Rio Grande*, Tippett's *A Child of Our Time*; from Europe, Honegger's *King David*, Orff's *Carmina Burana* and some interesting shorter works such as Kodaly's *Missa Brevis* and *Psalmus Hungaricus*, and Stravinsky's *Symphony of Psalms*. It is when we look at the post-war period: 1945 to the present day – that there seems to be a scarcity of choral works for enterprising societies keen to give an airing to contemporary music. Two works spring to mind, both often performed and both brilliant in their very different ways: Bernstein's *Chichester Psalms* and Poulenc's *Gloria*. But they last for only about 20 and 25 minutes respectively. Where are we to look for the larger-scale works which can form the centrepiece of an evening's entertainment?

The decay of oratorio as a musical art form has already been referred to; and as the 20th century progressed, its terminal illness began to be apparent. One probable reason was the association of oratorio with religion: hardly a plus-point in an age when religious belief had become, or was fast becoming, the exception rather than the norm. But oratorio-type works could of course be, and often were, set to non-religious texts; and a more important factor was the emergence of a musical language light-years away from anything the average untrained choralist could either comprehend or be expected to sing: the "avant-garde advanced so far as to be virtually out of sight" deplored in the earlier pages of this chapter. Taking one consideration with another it is easy enough to understand the lack of incentive felt by composers to undertake the hard work, and publishers the financial risk, involved in the production of substantial oratorio-like works.

Britten's *War Requiem* was commissioned: a large-scale choral work was asked for to celebrate the consecration of Coventry's new St Michael's Cathedral in 1962. But in all other respects it was a notable exception standing out like a Matterhorn in the Chilterns. How rare it was (and still is) and how refreshing, to come across a work of this kind by a contemporary composer, of any nationality, which is immediately acclaimed by both critics and the public as a profoundly moving masterpiece and which uses moreover a musical language undeniably 'modern' but still within range, still accessible.

In short, the *War Requiem* is a modern work whose difficulties are well worth tackling. But the Allied High Command planning the invasion of Normandy (a comparison suggested by the work's title) hardly needed to take a longer or more careful look at strategy and organisation. Apart from the resources called for: a chamber group as well as a large orchestra, organ and boys' choir, the mixed-choir members should be warned that although the music is not of frantic difficulty it can be a bit daunting and unrewarding to rehearse the chorus part on its own, as it were, with only a piano accompaniment. To prevent about half of them dropping out – as happened in my own experience with a smallish choir which attempted this work some years ago – they should be heartened with the promise of *rich rewards* which will surely come in the final rehearsals and the performance, when the orchestra and the soloists and the boys' choir play and sing the glorious stuff Britten has written for them, and the whole thing comes together and everybody feels it was an immensely worthwhile and exciting experience.

Might it also be helpful if the copies could be bought rather than rented so that the work can be rehearsed for more than one season, perhaps occupying the first half of the rehearsal time, with the second half devoted to a more familiar or less demanding work? (I have known this done, successfully, not with the *War Requiem* but with Bach's B minor Mass, the choir in question being comprised of university students, very few of whom had ever sung the work before.)

There are of course some other larger-scale works written since the war which have been taken on board by amateur choirs; but really very few, considering the period in question is more than 50 years. Worth mentioning are Maurice Duruflé's *Requiem:* a work which in recent years has 'gone up in the charts' to a point where it rivals the *Requiem* of Gabriel Fauré, which in some respects it resembles; Britten again, with his *St Nicholas* cantata; Vaughan Williams' *Hodie*, (already mentioned); and Herbert Howells' *Hymnus Paradisi.* Less well known, and more demanding, are: Racine Fricker's *Vision of Judgment,* which made a strong impression when it was first performed at the Leeds Festival in 1958; Anthony Milner's *The Water and the Fire*; and David Fanshawe's *African Sanctus*, which calls for an impressive assembly of congas, tom-toms, tam-tams, rock drum kit, amplified guitars and various other novelties unlikely to please traditionalists. Of Michael

Tippett's *The Mask of Time*, which appeared in 1982, two things need to be said: first, that it is a remarkable work; and second, that it is a long way beyond the reach of any but a very few amateur choirs.

While the general picture is one of bewildering variety, with the complete absence of anything that could be called a common musical language, there have been hopeful signs in the past 15 or 20 years of what might be very loosely called a more traditional style of choral composition. John Tavener demands mention in this context, as does the somewhat younger Scottish composer James MacMillan. Their interesting and original music has won wide acclaim but it tends to be imbued with a deep religious feeling – it could be called quasi-liturgical – reflecting strong allegiance to, respectively, the Greek Orthodox and Roman Catholic faiths. For obvious reasons this can produce difficulties, though not insuperable ones.

This fairly rapid survey of the contemporary musical scene can end very appropriately with a mention of John Rutter, most if not all of whose music has been written with young people and amateur choirs in mind. Some of us have suffered from over-exposure to his settings of Christmas carols, but it would be a pity for this to inhibit enjoyment of, for example, the fine and moving – and in places quite difficult – music of the *Requiem*, or the brilliant writing for brass, percussion and organ which accompanies the *Gloria*. Rutter is not another Benjamin Britten; but as with Britten, some gratitude would seem to be in order. We are lucky to have him.

Turning now from the music to the singers – in this context the members of amateur choral societies – let us first consider one distressingly salient fact: the high proportion, in so many of them, of balding pates, greying hair and matronly figures. How far into the 21st century, we wonder, can this ancient doddering lot possibly last? And who is going to replace them? Of course there are exceptions, there are borderline cases, a few younger faces can usually be picked out. But in general the recruitment of young people into choral singing remains a problem which is not going to go away.

Part of the trouble – probably a large part – is the diminishing importance attached to singing, if not to music in general, in maintained schools; in connection with which one can hardly avoid noting the terribly stark contrast with the private or fee-paying sector. Even in the bad old days when the so called public schools – especially those for boys – were largely in the grip of philistinism and games-worship, music making of various kinds went on in most of them, and there were some who offered music scholarships. Now that such schools have changed to the extent that they could almost be called junior universities, extremely high – not to say lavish – standards of music provision have become the norm.

But in the state sector things have tended to move disastrously in the opposite direction. One hears of large comprehensives being unable to offer music even as a GCSE option, let alone at A level. There seems to have been in recent decades a sort of 'dumbing-down' of music and of the arts in general. After all, what they offer cannot be quantified; value, as distinct from use, is not measurable, the arts contribute nothing to the Gross Domestic Product; computer literacy is much more important. So much that used to be taken for granted seems to have gone by the board: in particular class singing – even for just one or two not very long periods in the week.

At the risk of indulging in large generalisations supported by insufficient evidence, it could be true to say that the way forward is for choral societies to get involved in some way with schools and local communities: starting from the premiss that coming together to sing is a kind of basic human activity in a different category from other hobbies, interests and 'leisure activities'; that it is 'doing what comes naturally' and can be enjoyed by everyone except the tone deaf – who are a very small minority.

Basic musical literacy is of course needed; and this in turn needs some policy or plan for attracting and training youngsters, not to mention the services of dedicated and enthusiastic choir trainers prepared to give the time and effort. An impressive example of how such difficulties can be overcome is provided by Halifax Choral Society, which has established not only a Young Singers junior choir of almost 100 strong but also a Singing for Fun group of younger children aged between four and nine years (after which they graduate to the Young Singers). They are taught by the celebrated 'Kodaly method': essentially a back-to-basics approach with an emphasis on choral singing, on folk music, and on the importance of starting musical training in the primary school at the age of about six.

Probably Halifax is to some extent a special case, with an exceptionally strong and long established choral tradition as well as the resources of a fairly large city, with very large ones – Bradford and Huddersfield –

within easy distance. But even if the Halifax example cannot in all respects be emulated, could not something along the same lines be attempted here and there?

There are special circumstances, too, about another example; but it is different in most other respects. A large (500 pupils) independent girls' school situated in a Sussex village was until recently served by a music director of exceptional ability who fulfilled, over a period of nearly 30 years, a laudable ambition to introduce the girls to the great choral masterpieces rather than subsist on arrangements and on the small handful of standard works written for treble voices only. For this, adult singers were of course needed: tenors, basses and altos (the girls took only the soprano line). At first, only about a couple of dozen experienced singers came along to support the girls; but the choir eventually grew to a total of near 200 voices, with the adult members coming from as far as 15 or 20 miles away. (The whole enterprise was made possible by the Age of the Motor Car; the village is not well served by public transport.)

As for the girls, they were organised into a senior choir of 36 members drawn from the Fifth and Sixth Forms, who were auditioned annually; and a junior one comprising younger children who, after class singing tuition, augmented the senior choir when works written wholly or partly for double choir or SSATB were performed. The choir became widely known for its pure treble sound, keen intonation and near-professional competence. It undertook broadcasts and countrywide recitals, and commissioned works from contemporary composers as eminent as Kenneth Leighton, Alan Ridout and Bernard Rose. The retirement of the music director and some organisational changes at the school have made it unlikely to continue in exactly the same form. But its recent history certainly provides an example of the successful co-operation of a school with the local community – or more accurately in this case, with the outside world.

Money, money, money... so important, but depressing to write about, especially when it brings us up against problems which seem virtually insuperable. In order to survive, choral societies must attract audiences as well as singers; but it seems with every year that passes more difficult to do so. Friends and relatives of the performers can still be relied on to turn up: their sisters and their cousins may be reckoned up in dozens (and their aunts). But hundreds, not dozens, are needed to fill the hall and pay for the orchestra and the soloists and the rest of the multitudinous debit items that give the hard pressed Hon. Treasurer so many sleepless nights. How many societies rely on *Messiah* and on carol concerts at Christmas to recoup losses incurred over the rest of the year? 'Used to rely' would probably reflect the current situation more accurately: even this source shows signs of drying up. Some societies persuade their members to pay ever higher subscriptions; but obviously there must be a limit to this.

The root cause of the trouble is almost certainly the obvious one about which nothing can be done: the number of counter-attractions now offered, not just in large conurbations but in moderately sized or even small towns. One such attraction – it is hardly a matter for regret – is once again the local cinema: closed 30 years ago but recently re-opened or re-located with multiple screens offering a choice to suit all tastes. There is also the easy accessibility of superb performances of music on radio, CD recordings and sometimes television. Why pay money and turn out at a possibly inconvenient time to hear the local choral society put on what may be a less than inspiring performance of, say, the Brahms *Requiem* when an excellent recording can be picked up on a cheap CD label for about five pounds? This, though, is less certain as a factor contributing to audience decline. Live performances do of course have something to offer which is lacking in broadcasts or recordings.

Be that as it may, a more fruitful line of enquiry is simply: how can money be raised? Some local authorities will make grants more or less unconditionally; unlike the Arts Council and similar organisations who will note what they consider to be an unenterprising repertoire: too many old familiar favourites and not enough modern works (or less known ones of previous centuries); and they conclude the society is not worth supporting.

It is useless to try and point out that a grant is needed precisely to make possible the performance of music which will attract only small audiences.

Sponsorship by local commercial firms can be a lifeline; but the feasibility of this varies so much from place to place, it is difficult to make any helpful generalisations. For many societies a more secure source of funding is a system involving not just a few wealthy sponsors or patrons but a larger number of 'friends' who, in return for a not too daunting annual subscription, are offered various advantages and perks: in particular priority booking of good seats at reduced prices.

Much if not all of this will be stale news to most

treasurers. A book which begins with praise and appreciation of choir directors can fittingly end with an equally whole-hearted eulogy of the competent and dedicated society treasurer; whose task, though very different, is no less onerous and hardly less important.